SKI

SCHOOL

SKI SCHOOL

NH
NEW
HOLLAND

DAVID ANDERSON

First published in 2007 by
New Holland Publishers Ltd
London • Cape Town • Sydney • Auckland
www.newhollandpublishers.com

Garfield House
86–88 Edgware Road
London W2 2EA
United Kingdom

80 McKenzie Street
Cape Town 8001
South Africa

Unit 1, 66 Gibbes Street
Chatswood, NSW 2067
Australia

218 Lake Road
Northcote, Auckland
New Zealand

ISBN 978 1 84537 171 5

Publishing managers: Claudia dos Santos, Clare Hubbard
Commissioning editor: Alfred LeMaitre
Senior editor: Sarah Goulding
Designers: Maryna Beukes, Roland Codd
Illustrators: Steven Felmore, Stephen Dew
Production: Marion Storz

Reproduction by Pica Digital Pte Ltd, Singapore
Printed and bound in Malaysia by Times Offset (M) Sdn Bnd

10 9 8 7 6 5 4 3 2 1

NOTE: The author and publishers have made every effort to ensure that
all instructions given in this book are safe and accurate, but they cannot
accept liability for any resulting injury or loss or damage to either property
or person, whether direct or consequential and howsoever arising.

CONTENTS CONTENTS

CONTENTS CONTENTS

INTRODUCTION

"Powder snow skiing is not fun. It's life, fully lived, life lived in a blaze of reality".

Dolores LaChapelle

"The first fall of snow is not only an event, it is a magical event".

John Ruskin

You are never going to learn to ski simply from reading a book – and who would want to? The whole joy of skiing is being out in a winter alpine environment with a few good friends, snow crystals glinting in the sunlight, magnificent mountain panoramas all around, and a lovely long downhill laid out beneath you.

Books such as this are a huge help, however, enabling you to become an experienced skier much more quickly than if you were to try to get there all on your own. It doesn't matter whether you're a complete beginner or a seasoned expert – everyone can benefit from reminding themselves of the theory behind the practice.

Skiing in theory is as simple as a sport could be – you slide down snowy slopes on a pair of skis. But of course there's rather more to it than that, and it can be very daunting the first time you take to the hills. Even getting the right gear can be tricky, let alone using it properly.

In this book we take you from the complete basics, such as renting skis and boots, through to your first moves on skis, how to develop your technique as a beginner, and then how to move on to more advanced skills and more challenging terrain.

As you become a more proficient skier, you'll also discover that the sport is actually about rather more than just tearing downhill on snow. From wild half pipe action and backcountry telemarking, to alpine touring, hitting the moguls, racing and free riding, there are branches of skiing to appeal to everyone, whatever their age.

And once you get into skiing it means that, unlike other people, you can actually look forward to the winter. Planning your ski holiday is all part of the fun, and we've included a few tips on this, as well as ideas on where to go.

Read *Ski School* before you hit the slopes and take it with you on your ski holiday for a little bedtime reading (if you can stay awake). It will help you to become a competent skier that much more quickly and have even more fun on the mountain.

And that essentially is what skiing is all about – having fun. Whether your skills develop no further than the basic techniques described in chapter four, or you one day end up tearing apart super-steep backcountry slopes, who cares? Enjoying yourself is all that matters.

DAVID ANDERSON, 2007

GETTING STARTED

PEOPLE HAVE BEEN SKIING FOR THOUSANDS OF YEARS IN ONE FORM OR ANOTHER, BUT IT'S ONLY IN THE LAST CENTURY THAT SKIING HAS BECOME A SERIOUS RECREATIONAL SPORT. NOW, MODERN EQUIPMENT AND TECHNIQUES CAN HAVE YOU SKIING COMPETENTLY IN A MATTER OF DAYS.

Skiing dates back some 4,500 years, with short, wide, rudimentary wooden skis from this period having been found in a peat bog in Hoting, Sweden. Rock carvings from around the same time, discovered near Rödöy in northern Norway, show two figures using skis and poles to hunt elk. These ancient skis were designed for travelling and hunting across snowbound landscapes, and it is likely that similar implements were used throughout Eurasia, although snowshoes appear to have been favoured in the Americas.

It wasn't until the 18th and 19th centuries that skis were used for recreation. The Telemark and Christiania (now Oslo) areas of Norway were the first to introduce ski competitions (hence the eponymous 'telemark' and 'christie' methods of turning on skis). These competitions involved downhill and cross-country ski racing and ski jumping, all of which are still popular today.

Early skis were made of wood and were much more cumbersome than the lightweight models of today.

The earliest clubs devoted to competitive skiing were formed in Norway in the 1860s, followed by ski clubs in California (1867), Stockholm (1879), Munich (1891), Glarus, Switzerland (1893), the Ski Club of Great Britain (1903) and Kosciusko Alpine Club, Australia (1909). It's interesting that, after 4,500 years of skis being used for purely practical purposes, it took only 40 years for their use for sport and recreation to spread across the globe.

The sport of downhill skiing took hold in the European Alps in the early 20th century, largely through the influence of well-heeled British travellers. It was helped along by the development of 'fixed heel' bindings (mounted to the boot at both toe and heel), which gave more control on the steeper Alpine slopes than the traditional Telemark binding, which is only fixed at the toe.

The concept of the package ski holiday was introduced by Sir Arnold Lunn who, in 1898, organized a tour to the French Alps for 45 Britons. In 1928 Lunn was also responsible, along with the Ski Club of Great Britain, for organizing the infamous Inferno Downhill, the oldest surviving downhill ski race in the world.

The first Winter Olympics were held in Chamonix in 1924, and the Fédération Internationale de Ski (FIS) was established in the same year. However, the Olympics didn't include downhill skiing until the 1936 Games, held in Garmisch-Partenkirchen, Germany. Prior to that, the ski events comprised cross-country skiing and ski jumping.

Now that people who had little or no mountain background were getting into skiing, it was only natural that facilities were developed to cater for them. Beside the obvious hotels and chalets, ski lessons started in St Anton, Austria, with Hannes Scheider of the Arlberg Ski Club founding the world's first ski school in 1922. His techniques were used around the world until the 1960s, when Frenchman Jean-Claude Killy developed new learning methods. Although both Schneider and Killy's techniques have largely been superseded there are elements of both men's teaching methods which still influence modern skiing.

Today we take ski lifts for granted, but they were only invented in the 1930s. Prior to this, skiers had to hike up the slopes they wished to ski down. Ironically, this form of skiing is enjoying a renaissance as more and more experienced skiers head out into the back country under their own steam. The first 'drag lift' was built in 1934, followed two years later by the first chair lift (based on a banana boat hoist) in Sun Valley, Idaho. More advanced cable cars and multi-person chair lifts then began to appear in ski resorts around the world.

Immigrants from Scandinavia and Europe were instrumental in helping to develop skiing as a sport in Canada and the USA, both in the northeast and throughout the Rocky Mountains, where many former mining towns grew into ski resorts. As with Europe, traditional spa towns also discovered a new and lucrative winter market.

Throughout the mountain regions, new resorts were built from scratch. The privately-funded development of Sun Valley, Idaho began in the 1930s. Major French resorts, such as Tignes, Val Thorens and Avoriaz, were developed in the 1960s and '70s with government backing. Alongside resort development came technological advances such as 'grooming machines' (or 'piste bashers') to give the perfect corduroy pistes beloved of all skiers, and snowmaking machines for the times when nature isn't co-operating.

Equipment also steadily developed. Traditional leather boots were replaced by plastic ski boots in the 1970s, along with more efficient bindings, both of which helped to reduce the broken legs and ankles that were once a common ski injury – now thankfully quite rare. Around the same time, skis changed from long, heavy, wooden planks to shorter, lighter objects made from various hi-tech materials. In the 1990s, even shorter, wider, 'shaped' skis were introduced. These made the whole process of learning and improving far easier – and effectively means that you can now learn to ski reasonably competently in little more than the time it takes to read this book.

Through the 1980s and '90s breathable, water-proof fabrics were developed for ski wear that were lighter, warmer and more comfortable than anything that had gone before.

ALPINE VERSUS NORDIC

There are two basic 'families' of modern-day skiing: Alpine (or downhill) skiing and Nordic (or cross-country) skiing. Alpine skiing is what most people mean when they refer to 'skiing', although it actually originally developed from Nordic skiing, which it has effectively pushed into the shadows over the course of the last century. Like any healthy family, skiing has continued to expand to encompass various race disciplines, freestyle and freeskiing, moguls and ski jumping, as well as recreational specialities such as back country ski-ing, tree skiing, heliskiing and catskiing. All of these diffferent variations are examined in more detail over the following pages.

SKI THE WORLD

• *Around the world there are more than 6,000 ski areas in over 70 countries, ranging from huge, multi-lift resorts such as France's Val d'Isère and Whistler in Canada, to tiny one- or two-lift local hills, like Snowhaven in Idaho.*
• *Of these ski areas, over 600 are in Austria, while the USA, Germany and Japan have over 500 each and Sweden over 400. France, Switzerland and Italy each have in excess of 300 (although the latter three countries tend to have much larger ski areas).*
• *Less well-known countries where you can ski include Iran, India, Portugal, Morocco, Greece, Cyprus, Lebanon, Turkey and South Africa.*

Ski touring is a wonderful way to explore the winter landscape; just make sure you are fully prepared for the weather.

Nordic/cross-country skiing

As the name suggests, Nordic skiing developed in Scandinavia as a means of travelling across snow-bound winter landscapes. Modern-day Nordic skiing is the successor to what is effectively the ancestor of all skiing techniques, and for the residents of this lovely part of the world is still what they mean when they refer to 'skiing'.

Nordic skiing is essentially all about moving lightly and quickly across the landscape, as opposed to hurtling down it, as in Alpine skiing. Nordic ski trails are predominantly flat or undulating and the sport revolves around endurance since you propel yourself across the landscape and, when confronted by a hill, you have to climb it under your own steam – no mechanized ski lifts here!

Many Nordic skiers will tell you that not only is their sport the 'original' form of skiing, it relies far less on hi tech equipment. Nordic skis are thin and lightweight, with light bindings that are loose at the heel to allow your feet to lift and assist with propulsion. Nordic ski boots are like slippers compared to downhill boots, and are easy and relatively comfortable to walk in as well as ski in. Other Nordic equipment also tends to be quite minimalist. The lightweight ski poles are longer than downhill poles to allow for more 'thrust', since the poles are used to assist forward movement, while lighter clothing is worn, since you burn more energy when Nordic skiing and don't need to wear as much clothing to keep warm.

As with Alpine skiing, Nordic trails are graded for difficulty, and can vary from just a few kilometres to tens of kilometres in length. Regions such as the beuatiful Peer Gynt ski area in Norway have trail

The light, narrow skis used in Nordic skiing make it easy to move along valleys and through forests.

systems that can be linked to cover huge distances, and keen Nordic skiers may undertake multi-day trips, spending nights in cosy ski huts along the trail.

The trails are invariably groomed to allow for easier use, along similar principles to the grooming used on downhill trails, although the machines are considerably smaller and the trails themselves impact far less on the landscape than downhill pistes. Most big ski resorts have some Nordic trails, usually at lower elevations than the Alpine trails, and set apart from them as well. The trails invariably pass through the quiet forest and woodland areas in the valleys beneath the main peaks, although in Scandinavia there are trails that run through the high, undulating upland areas.

Racing is a big part of Nordic skiing – indeed, Nordic racing was introduced to the Winter Olympics 12 years before downhill racing made its debut. Race distances vary from 5 km (3 miles) to 50 km (30 miles) or more.

The basics of Nordic skiing can be picked up over a weekend and, in terms of pure exercise, there are few sports that give you such a good total workout (and even fewer that take you through such magnificent landscapes at the same time).

You move forward through a combination of a kick-step with one foot and a gliding step with the other. Your ski pole is planted down as the opposite leg performs a kick off. Slight variations to this basic technique allow you to travel up and down inclines. Downhills are more difficult to negotiate than on alpine skis because Nordic skis are much narrower, don't have metal edges to bite into the snow, and the bindings don't provide as much support as those on alpine skis. A more rapid form of travel is possible using a skating technique: a side-to-side motion pushing off the inside of the skis while 'poling' – using ski poles to push forward.

If the conditions are poor for Alpine skiing, or if you want to try something different, Nordic is worth a try – after all, the more types of skiing you master, the more fun you can have in winter.

Alpine/downhill skiing

This essentially consists of sliding downhill on a pair of skis. An estimated 70 per cent of all snowsports enthusiasts get their kicks on downhill skis. Some traditionalists argue that it's not as 'pure' a form of skiing as Nordic. It relies more on infrastructure and has a greater impact on the environment, from ski lifts and groomed trails, to large ski lodges and the use of energy-intensive processes in the manufacture of equipment.

Alpine, or downhill, skiing is exhilarating and relatively easy to learn.

Competitive ski racing is an adrenaline-filled, high-speed, hectic race for the finish line. It is exhilarating to watch – and even more so for the participants. Here, skier-cross competitors fight it out.

Ski racing

In the same manner that Alpine skiing developed from Nordic skiing, so other ski disciplines have sprung up on the back of Alpine skiing. The most obvious of these is racing, which is broken down into the four disciplines practised in the Winter Olympics and on the World Cup ski circuit.

Downhill

This is pretty much a matter of seeing who can ski down a set course in the fastest possible time. A downhill course has an altitude difference of between 500 and 1,000 m (1,640–3,280 ft) for men and 500–800 m (1,640–2,624 ft) for women,

and is prepared by hard-packing the snow until it becomes little more than ice, which gives faster speeds. Top racers will reach speeds of 130 kph (80 mph) or more on the faster sections of the course. The gates (marker poles) that racers must pass through are wide and well-spaced, and are more to define the route down the mountain as opposed to being obstacles that the skier must negotiate (as with slalom races).

Slalom

Originating from a Norwegian word meaning 'sloping track', the slalom involves racing down a very tight course between gates – racers must pass through all of these; if any are missed they're disqualified. Run over a much shorter course than the downhill, the slalom has between 55 and 75 gates for men (40–60 for women) along a course that averages around 550 m (1,804 ft) in length with a vertical drop of 180–220 m (590–722 ft) for men and 140–200 m (459–656 ft) for women. The gradient is far steeper than it appears when watching a race on television. A slalom event is run over two different courses, with the best combined time for both courses determining the winner.

Giant Slalom (GS)

As the name implies, this is a bigger version of the standard slalom, run over a course of around 1.5 km (one mile) in length with a vertical drop of 300–400 m (984–1,312 ft). Competitors race twice and the best combined time determines the winner.

Super Giant Slalom (Super G)

This is a mix of giant slalom and downhill, involving long, wide turns through a set course with a vertical drop of 300–450 m (984–1,476 ft) for men and 300–400 m (984–1,312 ft) for women, with the winner decided on the basis of one run.

The Combined

The combined is made up of races over downhill as well as slalom runs, with the cumulative time over both runs deciding the winner.

Become a ski racer

If you are keen to learn the basics of ski racing, there are many resorts that have timed courses for recreational skiers, where you can either compete against the clock or against friends on gated courses. You can even take race-specific lessons to pick up a few tips on how to get down the course more quickly.

Besides being exciting and fun, racing down a steep course helps you to improve and develop useful skiing skills and techniques and gain confidence on trickier terrain. In particular, you have to learn to look ahead and plan your route down the mountain; to use your skiing skills more efficiently to improve your time down the course; and to turn where the course dictates rather than where you might prefer.

Contestant on the Super Giant Slalom (Super G) course.

DIFFERENT TYPES OF SKIING

Expert skiers invariably find that there is some aspect of the sport that appeals most, be it bouncing through a mogul field (see below) or heading off into the wild blue yonder on an off-piste ski trip. Here are the options that are available once you become more accomplished.

Freestyle

Freestyle skiing consists of a variety of disciplines, including the dual and single mogul events.

Single moguls

The aim is to ski as fast and stylishly as possible down a steep slope (up to 32 degrees) covered in moguls (bumps). These may be as big as a car. Two different aerial manoeuvres, off specially built launch pads, are performed on the way down the course. Scoring is based on the stylishness of the skiing, the time for the run and the difficulty of the jumps.

Dual moguls

A head-to-head race between two skiers down the same course, involving the same criteria as single moguls.

Ripping through a competitive mogul field is a challenge even for experienced skiers.

Aerials

The name is self-explanatory for an event that will see top competitors getting up to 15 m (50 ft) of air from specially constructed ramps (kickers). They execute a series of somersaults, twists, etc. before landing on an extremely steep slope. Points are awarded for take-off, style and landing.

Freeriding

Freeriding is a spin-off from freestyle and has been influenced by snowboarding. It consists of jump events using half pipes (the newest World Cup discipline), quarter pipes and table tops to perform spectacular flips, spins and grabs. These are helping to push the limits of what is possible on skis, especially in the air.

Also in the freeride stable is skier-cross (another World Cup discipline), in which four skiers race together down a very tight mini-downhill course which has a variety of features built in, including jumps, turns, hits and rollers, the aim being to finish first. Crashes and collisions are common, making it a popular spectator sport.

Freeskiing

Freeskiing is the sport of skiing 'the whole mountain' and not restricting yourself to what is available on the pistes within a resort boundary. Cynics might say this is what was once known as off-piste or back country skiing. However, there's a little more to it, in that freeski practitioners also head for natural jumps, kickers and steeper terrain. In effect, the best freeskiers are pushing the limits of what can be done outside the boundaries of resorts.

Freeskiing is the ultimate off-piste experience, but you need expert skills and the ability to take care of yourself in difficult situations.

Back country/off-piste skiing

Back country, or off-piste, skiing has some overlap with freeskiing, but this is more for ordinary mortals who don't wish to leap off 15 m (50 ft) cliffs and race down 45-degree slopes when they're out in the back country.

You can hike to the back country or use ski lifts to access it, but the attractions are obvious – fresh, untracked snow and pristine, secluded mountain environments. However, you need plenty of mountain experience, the proper equipment and good skiing skills, to be able to head off safely into the back country. Avalanche rescue techniques, navigation and first aid skills are all standard requirements unless you employ the services of a guide (this applies to freeskiing as well).

Heli- and catskiing

For those who don't want to physically climb the slopes they wish to ski down, other options include heliskiing (helicopter-assisted ascents) and catskiing (snowcat, or piste groomer-assisted ascents), both of which depend on the size of your wallet. Two days of heliskiing can easily cost as much as a week of regular skiing and, while catskiing is considerably cheaper, it is still much more costly than lift-accessed skiing. However, both options provide effortless access to remote, unpeopled slopes where untracked powder awaits you, with skilled guides to ensure that you ski in safety, plus the thrill of one or more helicopter lifts into the mountains (snowcats are also fun if not quite so exciting). And, as a bonus, your accommodation may be a luxury mountain lodge, often situated miles away from any other sign of human life.

Below *Helicopters can deliver you to some of the best virgin powder, but they are expensive and not exactly eco-friendly.*

Opposite *Even die-hard skiers can learn to enjoy the tricks and challenges of snowboarding.*

Ski jumping

If you ever get the chance to go to the top of a ski jump, as I once did at Lake Placid in New York State, do so – then stand and wonder what would make someone ever want to ski down one.

The vertiginous slope of the jump tower is as high as an apartment block, the drop at the end is as high as another tower block and the landing zone is steeper than many black runs.

Assuming you survive all this steepness and fresh air, you'll be scored on the distance you cover and the style with which you do it. Skilled jumpers will travel over 100 m (328 ft) and remain in the air for up to seven seconds.

Originating in Scandinavia, ski jumping remains a big part of the culture there, with jumps such as the one at Holmenkollen in Norway attracting over a million visitors a year. There's also a 'Nordic combined' event, a Scandinavian tradition, comprising a ski jumping and Nordic skiing contest in which the combined results determine the winner.

Snowboarding

The best things about snowboarding are that you wear soft boots that are more comfortable than rigid ski boots; it's easier to learn than skiing; it's immense fun; and it's easier than skiing when heading into deep powder.

Once the 'new kid' on the slopes, snowboarding is gradually being overtaken by skiing as the 'cool' winter sport. Ironically, this is largely due to the appropriation of elements of snowboard design by ski manufacturers, which have helped to make modern skis easier to learn on, ski on and do tricks on. As a result, skiers are now riding the half pipe and off-piste (both at one time the home ground of snowboarders) with as much, if not more, style than boarders.

However, the fact that skiing is somewhat harder to learn means that snowboarding will always remain popular – although only 20 per cent of snowsport enthusiasts world wide are estimated to be boarders).

APRÈS-SKI

For many skiers, après-ski is almost as much a part of their holiday as the actual skiing, and many resorts focus on their bars, clubs, restaurants and other entertainment facilities to attract visitors.

Whether you want to chill out with a quiet drink in a traditional alpine bar, or rip it up until 4am in a club, these and pretty much any other option you can think of will be available in one resort or another. One thing to beware of, however, is that the effects of alcohol are more pronounced at altitude and can also be influenced by a hard day of physical activity on the slopes. Furthermore, if you do drink too much, you may not be up to skiing the next day. If you have paid a lot of money for a skiing holiday, it is as well to remember that, while you can drink any time at home, your skiing time is limited, so take it easy if you want to stay fit for the slopes. If you are planning a party night it may be worth checking the weather forecast first, because if fresh snow is forecast overnight you might want to change your plans in order to stay sharp for the following day.

Not all après-ski revolves around alcohol, of course. Many ski resorts offer all sorts of activities once the lifts are closed, from the active – such as dog/horse/reindeer sledding, ice skating, floodlit cross-country skiing, bob sledding or snowmobiling – to the relaxing, such as saunas, massages, spa treatments and shopping (although much of what you buy in a ski resort will probably be cheaper in the nearest big town or back home).

The resort party scene may rock at night,
but remember that too little sleep and too much
alcohol can affect your skiing. If you are taking
a long-awaited ski holiday, it may be better
to tame the party animal – at least until you
get home!

ESSENTIALS

MODERN SKI GEAR, FROM SKIS AND BOOTS TO JACKETS AND GOGGLES, IS USER-FRIENDLY, COMFORTABLE AND LOOKS COOL – A FAR CRY FROM THE DAYS OF PASTEL JUMP SUITS. BUT IT PAYS TO GET THE BEST YOU CAN AFFORD TO ENSURE COMFORT AND SAFETY ON THE MOUNTAIN.

When planning a ski holiday, the short answer to the question 'what gear do I need?' is 'probably not as much as you think' – certainly when it comes to actually buying it. When starting out you should hire skis, poles and boots, and maybe even ski wear. However, if you enjoy the outdoors the chances are that, apart from one or two specialist items such as ski trousers and goggles, you probably already have most of what you need.

There are three main reasons for not buying all your ski gear before your first visit to the slopes:

- You may find that you don't actually like skiing (unlikely, but possible);
- You won't really know what you want until you've had some experience of the sport; and
- If you wait until you get to the slopes and hire your gear there you can always change your skis, boots etc. if they are not suitable.

Whether renting or buying, any good ski shop will help you choose your equipment, especially skis and boots, on the basis of your skiing experience, physique, fitness, age and budget. If you're not getting the help and advice you need, go elsewhere – there are plenty of ski shops around. Of course, you can always buy on the internet, often at a discount. That said, some kit, boots in particular, should never be bought untried and untested. Be wary of splashing out on a pair of skis over the web unless you've had the opportunity to ski the exact same model beforehand.

At almost all levels of skiing you'll be reliant on advice from ski shop staff as to what is best suited to you. Every season ski gear manufacturers release new designs, upgrades and tweaks to improve their products; well-informed shop staff should be up-to-date with all these improvements. Novices, in particular, need sound, easily understandable advice. Don't let the sales assistant baffle you with science and terminology; if you don't know what they're talking about, ask them to speak in plain English.

If you're renting your equipment at a ski resort you'll be able to change it if you don't feel happy with what you've got, which offers a great opportunity to try out different makes and models of ski, boots, bindings and so on to see what feels best.

BASIC SKI COMPONENTS

Skis

When it comes to skis, size matters! As a novice skier you ought to be riding skis that are slightly shorter than you are. In the beginning, your ski instructor and the rental shop will advise on the best length for you. By the time you're ready to buy your own skis you'll have a pretty good idea of the length on which you feel best.

As a rough rule of thumb when buying for the first time, the kind of skis you'd be renting after two to three weeks of skiing should see you through the next few seasons, until your skill levels are such that you need to think about upgrading. Don't go too long too soon, though. Longer skis are more difficult to control and turn and even expert skiers rarely use anything much longer than 180 cm (6 ft) these days, especially on piste.

Always try new skis before you buy them – 'demo' models should be available, but make sure they are the same length as the skis you may eventually purchase. You may be charged a rental fee to use demo skis, but this should be deducted from the price if you decide to buy those skis.

Try to test all the demo skis over the same terrain so you can get an accurate comparison of how they feel and perform. Bear in mind that different bindings will also change the feel.

If you are taking lessons, ask your instructor for his or her thoughts on skis you are trying out: feedback from professionals, who can see how you are skiing on different skis, is invaluable.

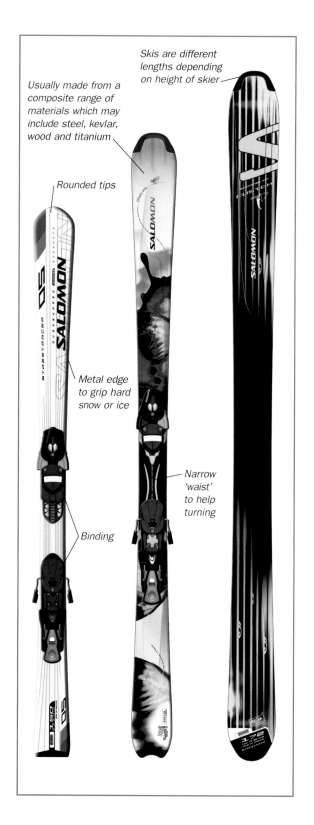

Usually made from a composite range of materials which may include steel, kevlar, wood and titanium

Skis are different lengths depending on height of skier

Rounded tips

Metal edge to grip hard snow or ice

Narrow 'waist' to help turning

Binding

A selection of modern skis from well-known French manufacturer Salomon.

Bindings

Bindings keep you and your skis together. A binding that doesn't work properly can be lethal. If they release too easily you'll end up falling on hard turns and steep terrain as your binding pops open. However, if they don't release easily enough you could damage your ankle, knee or leg in a bad fall as the ski twists and turns it.

As a beginner, you need a very basic binding, so there's no need to go overboard with costly hi-tech lightweight titanium models and riser plates (which allow for harder, more angulated turning). You can always put new bindings on your skis, and vice versa, if you decide to upgrade, although some manufacturers produce integrated ski and binding packages.

The ski shop will set up your bindings based on a small leaflet you'll fill in (and sign) detailing your weight, height, age and skiing ability. From this they will calculate the DIN setting for your bindings. 'DIN' stands for *Deutsche Industrie Normen*, and represents a universal setting used by ski manufacturers to determine the point at which the binding will release. Ask them to show you the DIN setting so that you know it for future reference.

When you buy bindings, you should look for one which, when set for you, has a setting midway between the bottom and top of that binding's DIN range – if you have to set it lower, then it is probably too high-end a binding for your ability (and will cost more); if you have to set it higher, it may not be robust enough for the skiing you plan to do on it.

A selection of modern bindings.

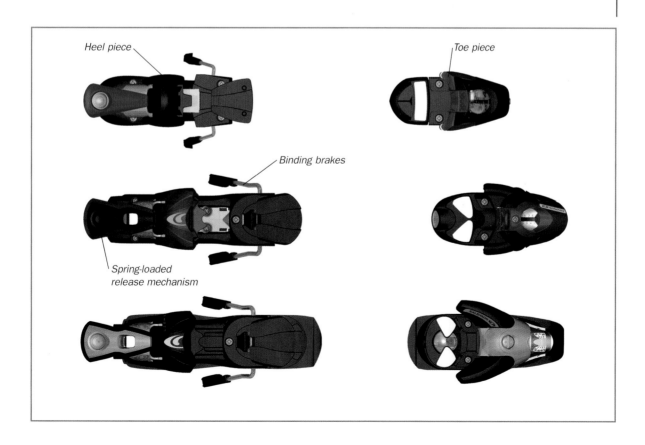

Heel piece

Toe piece

Binding brakes

Spring-loaded release mechanism

Poles

Your first rental poles may be somewhat bent and battered, and probably quite heavy. You may think it's no big deal but, when buying your own, go for the lightest pair you can afford. Over the course of a day the weight adds up and lighter poles make a difference. Furthermore, once you reach the stage of using them to assist with turns on steeper terrain, bumps, etc. it's better to have lightweight poles.

To ensure you have the right length of pole for your height, turn it upside down and grip it beneath the basket. Your forearm should be parallel with the ground when you do this.

The straps should be loose enough to get a gloved hand in and out of quickly and easily, although there's something to be said for not using straps at all. The reason for this is that in a fall you invariably put out your hands to absorb the impact; if the poles are attached to your wrist and you are holding the grip with your hands through the straps, your thumbs will take all the weight, leading to a strained, sprained or even broken thumb – one of the most common ski injuries. If your poles aren't strapped to your wrist this is less likely to happen. On the other hand, it may mean trudging back up the mountain to collect the poles you left behind in a spill – but then that's good exercise.

More expensive, lightweight poles are a bit of a luxury, but one worth having.

Boots

Getting the right ski boots is the most important step to enjoying your skiing – if your boots don't fit, and especially if they're uncomfortable or even painful, skiing can become a nightmare.

Boots should be the first piece of kit you buy once you get into skiing. You can rent skis to fit boots so, by owning your own, you can be sure your

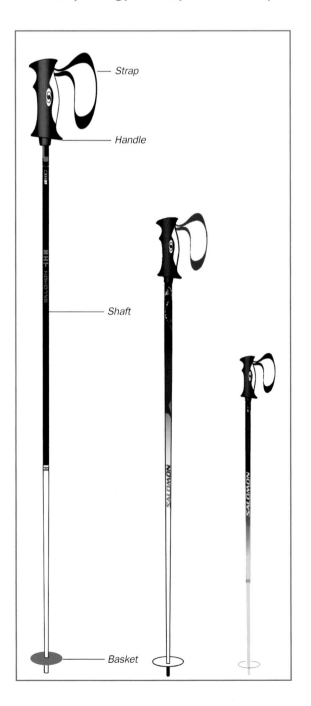

feet are comfortable every time you ski, which may not always be the case with rental boots.

Before you buy boots do plenty of research; visit ski shops, ask ski instructors and friends, read magazine reviews and check out the Internet to see what your options are. Then hit the ski shops and try on as many pairs as necessary until you find something that feels absolutely right.

This will probably be a long process, so give yourself a couple of hours or more, and your decision should be backed up by sound advice and assistance from a specialist technician who has been trained in fitting ski boots. Be honest about your skiing ability and try different makes and styles of boots designed for your level of skiing until you find something that fits snugly but comfortably around your foot, ankle and lower leg.

Most skiers use 'overlap entry' boots, which fasten over the top of your foot by means of a series of buckles. They can be tricky to get into, but provide good support for your foot and ankle and consequently give better performance.

You don't want too much movement in the heel, but neither do you want the boot to be too tight. Expect the boots to feel unwieldy at first – they are, after all, designed to provide support as you hurtle downhill at speed – but if they pinch, rub or chafe anywhere at all reject them. Some adjustments to fit can be made by inserting footbeds, which can be either off the peg or custom-made and may make a huge difference. A good boot fitter could spend all afternoon getting you the perfect fit, and should also offer you the option of additional fittings if the boot becomes uncomfortable after you've used it a few times.

It is worth taking the time to get your boots right because if your feet are happy when you're skiing, the rest of you will be happy as well – and you'll learn and improve much more quickly in well-fitting ski boots. Also remember that a well-fitted ski boot is not only comfortable, it will also keep your feet warm.

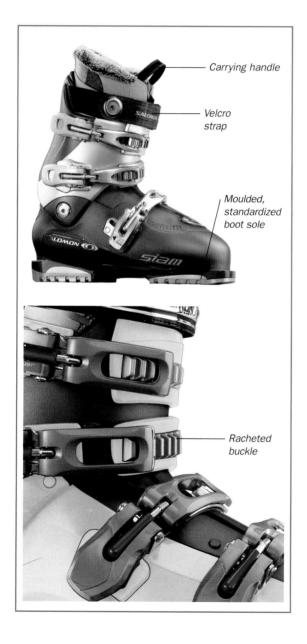

Carrying handle

Velcro strap

Moulded, standardized boot sole

Racheted buckle

A modern four-buckle ski boot. Comfortable boots are the key to enjoying your skiing.

CLOTHING AND ACCESSORIES

Layers

Staying dry and warm on the slopes is vital if you're to have a good day out, and it is relatively simple with modern hi-tech ski clothing. You need to dress in layers, using wicking and breathable fabrics. These move moisture (i.e. sweat) away from your body, but prevent snow, sleet or rain from getting in, thus keeping you dry and warm. Another advantage is that you can add or remove layers to adjust your body temperature as necessary.

The layer next to your skin – the base layer – should be light, thin and made of a high wicking material such as Helly Hansen's well-established Lifa fabric. Another excellent, if more expensive option, is merino wool. Whatever your choice, the base layer should be a reasonably snug fit, since

you don't want it bunching up under your clothes. Your layers should also include underwear and, that sexiest of garments, long johns.

Next is the mid-layer, ideally a mid-weight fleece, merino wool or a wool mix. If you opt for something that looks good for general wear, you can save luggage space. Note that in cold conditions you will probably require two mid-layers. Finally comes the outer layer, which should be waterproof, windproof and breathable, and cover both your upper and lower body. Choose a separate jacket and ski pants, which nowadays come in various designs. Ski jackets, in particular, can often be used as outdoor and leisure wear all year round.

Jacket

The ideal ski jacket should have features such as an ergonomic hood, a high collar to keep the wind out, plenty of zipped pockets, 'pit zips' (underarm zips for venting), Velcro cuff fastenings, a 'powder skirt' (an inner elasticated hem to prevent snow riding up inside the jacket when you fall) and an elasticated outer hem. Jackets come in different weights, from lightweight shells to heavier, insulated garments, so choose one to suit your taste and how much you feel the cold.

Trousers

Ski pants should also be waterproof, windproof, breathable and possibly insulated. Things to look out for are zipped pockets, zipped leg/crotch vents and elasticated or Velcro boot cuffs to hold the hems over your boots and prevent snow getting up inside. They should also be a reasonably loose fit for ease of movement.

With the right gear, your body will remain warm and dry, even when it starts snowing.

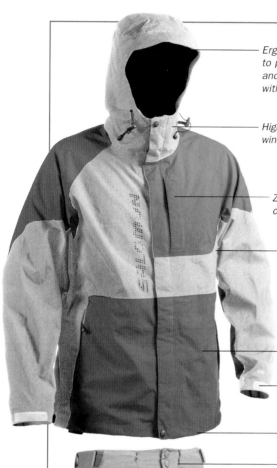

Ergonomic hood, shaped to provide maximum ear and face protection without restricting vision

High collar to keep out the wind and snow

Some of the basic features to look for in essential ski wear.

Zipped pockets for keys, cash and other valuables

Pit zips for underarm ventilation

Internal powder skirt

Velcro cuff fastenings to prevent snow from creeping in

Adjustable hem

Velcro adjustable waist

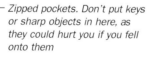

Zipped pockets. Don't put keys or sharp objects in here, as they could hurt you if you fell onto them

Zipped leg vents to keep you cool when things start to hot up on the slopes

Above *Windproof fleece – good mid-layer, or can be used as an outer layer on warm spring days.*
Top *Close-fitting thermal t-shirt, made to wick away moisture while retaining essential body heat close to the core.*

Velcro boot cuffs inside the outer leg

OTHER VITAL KIT

Skiing is a great sport if you like gear, with plenty of equipment you can persuade yourself into thinking is essential, even if it is not. The kit below is definitely essential, however.

- **Gloves** Buy the best ski gloves you can afford; you won't enjoy yourself if your hands feel cold all day. The best gloves come in breathable, waterproof fabrics, with an inner glove for added warmth and an elasticized or Velcro cuff to prevent snow from getting inside. Some people prefer mitts, which in theory are warmer since all your fingers remain together. If you suffer from poor circulation, look for gloves with built-in pouches for handwarmer packs.

- **Headwear** A good ski hat is essential, since you lose a vast amount of heat through your head. As far as fabric and design are concerned, it's a case of personal choice. Some hats come in Windstopper fleece which, as the name suggests, is windproof for additional warmth.

- **Protective helmets** These are a common sight on the slopes. Although modern helmets are lightweight and well ventilated, some people find them somewhat restrictive and/or too warm. It is a matter of choice, but novice skiers, who are likely to fall more than most, should consider wearing them. Once you have the ability to ski among the trees they are even more important – it goes without saying who will come off worst if you headbutt a Scots pine. In some ski resorts it is compulsory for children to wear ski helmets; and it's a good idea to provide them with a helmet even if this isn't the case.

- **Socks** Ski socks have technical features that allow them to flex with your feet and ankles, provide cushioning, wick away moisture and, most importantly, keep your toes warm. They're considerably more expensive than regular socks, but

A hat and gloves are essential to keep warm. It's worth buying the best gloves you can afford. A helmet is worth serious consideration – especially if you fall a lot!

since they keep your feet warm, dry and comfortable, they're a good investment, so go for the best you can afford. Make sure the socks are not too thick because this can restrict circulation and make your feet cold. Don't wear two pairs because they can get rucked up inside the boot, which is very uncomfortable – your ski boots should fit snugly with just one pair of socks. Choose socks which come all the way up to your knee for added warmth and also to prevent your bare shins from chafing against the front of your ski boots.

- **Eyewear** Sunglasses and/or goggles are essential to protect your eyes against the glare from the snow and the intense sunlight at high altitudes (see page 42). Choose good-quality lenses with UV protection and maybe a polarizing lens. Other than that, it is a matter of taste. If you wear prescription glasses, you can buy goggles to fit over them, but make sure you try them together to ensure a good fit. Alternatively, wear prescription sunglasses.

- **Goggles** These are especially useful when it's snowing; use a yellow, rose or red-tinted lens in these conditions to emphasize the land relief in poor light. I prefer to wear sunglasses in all but poor light or snowfall. However, if you're likely to fall often then goggles are a better option since snow can't get behind the lenses when you fall as it does with sunglasses. Goggles are also available with prescription lenses.

- **A good-quality cloth** This is useful for wiping lenses and preventing scratches. Don't wipe the inside of the lenses if they get snow, water or condensation on them – they are coated with a special anti-misting agent and you'll damage this. Rather let your goggles' lenses dry naturally to retain their anti-misting properties.

Goggles are vital when it's snowing and useful the rest of the time to protect your eyes against the sun.

Children often have a natural sense of balance and a lack of fear of falling that makes it easy for them to learn to ski.

BUYING TIPS

- *End-of-season sales can produce some great deals, both at the resort or back home, but you need to do your homework. Compare ski gear prices at foreign resorts with those at home – if monetary exchange rates are good you may find some bargains.*
- *If you have used, but functional, ski gear, ask whether part-exchange deals are possible when buying replacement kit.*
- *Check out the ski and outdoor magazines for gear reviews – they may have tested the kit you're thinking of buying.*

SKIING FOR KIDS

Most manufacturers make smaller skis specifically for children, with the same features as those of adults. The length should be about chin height, and the ski should bend under the weight of the child. This helps them to control their turns. It is essential to take weight, age, experience and ability into consideration when selecting skis.

This also applies to bindings – the setting should be neither too loose nor too tight. Ensure that children can get their boots in and out of the binding without too much difficulty.

Ski boot fit is as important for children as it is for adults, so use the services of a professional boot fitter. At first, you may need to reassure your child that ski boots are meant to be tight and somewhat restrictive compared with normal footwear.

Children should also be able to use the buckle system unassisted, since they may have to adjust them when you're not there to help.

Ski poles are an option rather than a necessity for complete beginner children. Many ski schools don't bother with them initially, since they're a distraction and can even be a hazard in falls, lift queues, etc. However, once your child is reasonably competent and ready to use poles, the same fitting criteria apply as for adults – they should just touch the ground when held upside-down at arm's length. Don't go for the budget option of buying poles for your child to 'grow into' as they'll be more difficult for them to use.

Skiing needs to be fun for kids if they're going to stick with it. If they're cold, tired and miserable they won't enjoy it and you won't enjoy them – so ensure that they don't overdo it.

Most ski resorts have kindergartens where professionals will look after your children on and off the slopes whilst you have some quality ski time for yourself.

ACCESSORIES

- **Rucksack** A small rucksack allows you to take along an extra layer of clothing, snacks, camera, wallet, keys, hydration pack or water bottle. Choose a snug fitting pack that's not too big and be aware that you may have to hold it on your lap on some chair lifts.

- **Heater packs** Heater packs for hands and feet are relatively inexpensive. The more expensive battery-operated boot warmers will keep the inside of your boots warm whilst skiing.

- **Walkie-talkie** A bit of a mountain toy really, but useful when skiing with friends and the party gets split up – and a lot cheaper than using a mobile phone (which may not always have a signal in the mountains anyway).

- **Ski bags** Skis are fairly sturdy bits of kit – and they need to be with the amount of wear they get on the mountain – but it's best to pack them in protective ski bags when you're travelling (many airlines require this). You can also put your poles and maybe a few items of clothing in with them, which will free up space in your travel bag. You can buy single, double or multi-ski bags of tough, abrasion-resistant material or lightweight plastics. Ski bags with wheels are easier to carry around airports and train stations.

- **Boot bags** A boot bag will enable you to take your boots onto the plane as hand luggage. That way there's no danger of you ending up in one resort and your boots in another.

- **Luggage** You'll be carrying a lot of gear with you on a ski trip, and it'll be quite heavy, so use a good solid bag that won't burst open or tear. A wheelie bag is worth considering for ease of transport.

- **Car roof carriers** If you're driving to the mountains, you'll need a roof rack of some sort. Lockable roof boxes allow you to carry a number of pairs of skis and poles along with other items. Roof bars aren't as thief-proof nor as aerodynamic, and also permit road grime to get into your bindings if your skis are not in a ski bag.

Ski and boot bags are essential when travelling with expensive ski gear.

35

TRAVEL TIPS

Getting there

Plane Check with the airline before flying that you can actually take your skis. It's unlikely they'll say no, but some restrict how many pairs you can put in one bag. There may also be a surcharge, especially with budget airlines and package tour operators.

Car Your car will need to be prepared for harsh winter conditions. In particular, ensure you have enough de-icer in the washer and anti-freeze in the radiator, and carry snow chains – in some places you won't be allowed up into the mountains without them. You should also take out overseas insurance cover for the vehicle and check on driving regulations in the countries you'll be travelling through. Bear in mind that bad winter weather may affect your journey, from delayed ferry crossings to fog, rain, snow or sleet whilst on the road. Ideally there should be two drivers to relieve the strain of the long journey.

As long as you prepare your car for winter conditions, you should have no problems.

Train Travelling overnight by train can give you one or two more days to ski than on a regular package holiday, as you can arrive on a Saturday morning and leave on the following Saturday night.

When to go

If you can ski outside 'peak season' it will be a lot cheaper. Peak season covers the Christmas and New Year holidays, school holidays (usually February) and Easter. January can have good snow and empty slopes, but shorter daylight hours and it's often very cold. March will see longer days, a good build up of snow on the mountains, and won't be too busy. April can be good in more snow sure resorts – there's still the possibility of fresh snowfall, and warm sunny days are not uncommon, offering superb afternoon skiing in spring snow.

When you're there

Lift passes

The cost of lift passes (or lift tickets) adds considerably to your ski holiday, and will vary a great deal between resorts and countries. 'Linked' resorts that have lift connections with other ski areas will have the option of a cheaper 'resort only' pass or a more expensive 'area' pass. There may be no point paying for an area pass if there's enough skiing in a single resort to keep you occupied all week.

Passes tend to work out cheaper if you buy them for longer periods, although if you don't ski all of the days on your pass you won't get a refund for those not used. Half-day passes are also available, but in most resorts they're only available from mid-day.

Lifts on nursery/beginner slopes are usually free for ski school students, and in many resorts young children can ski for free anywhere on the mountain as long as they're with an adult.

Insurance

Your insurance policy should cover you for damage to skis and luggage whilst travelling, theft, loss, accidents whilst in transit, etc. and most importantly, for evacuation from the mountain, medical treatment and repatriation in the event of an accident.

Shop around for your policy and don't automatically take the one you'll be offered by a travel agent when you book your holiday, as these can be relatively expensive.

If you do a lot of travelling consider an annual travel insurance policy, which can be cheaper, as well as preventing the hassle of having to take out a new policy every time you go abroad.

Ski schools and lessons

Two invaluable tips for first time skiers are:

1. Take lessons;
2. Take them from a qualified ski instructor and not your friend or partner – the latter is a great way to jeopardise a good relationship!

Ski schools don't generally vary too much in the quality of their teaching - instructors at all ski schools will have been through rigorous training programmes developed by national ski associations, so you can be sure you're getting totally professional coaching.

Private ski schools and clinics offer equally good coaching, usually but not exclusively aimed at more experienced skiers – a good example is the British run Development Clinic in Val d'Isere.

Some resorts are particularly known for the quality of their ski schools and for being especially good for novice skiers due to a combination of good learner slopes and good instructors. Good beginner resorts include Les Arcs and Flaine in France, Cervinia and Livigno in Italy, Mayrhofen in Austria, Soldeu-El Tartar in Andorra, Wengen in Switzerland, Geilo in Norway, Beaver Creek and Smuggler's Notch in the USA, and Sun Peaks and Stoneham in Canada.

For intermediates, good options include La Plagne, Alpe d'Huez and Serre Chevalier in France, Selva Gardena and Sestriere in Italy, Bad Gastein in Austria, Heavenly and Durango in the USA and Big White and Panorama in Canada.

Lessons can vary from one-to-one instruction from an hour to a full day, to group lessons, which usually run over a morning or afternoon. Both private and group lessons can be booked in packages of several days, which is cheaper than paying for individual days.

Naturally, private one-to-one lessons are more expensive, but you tend to progress more quickly. On the other hand, group lessons can be more fun and less intense, since it's enjoyable to share the trials, tribulations and laughs of learning with other people, and they are also a great way to make new friends.

A good way to start your ski career is to book a package of half-day morning lessons ('half day' lessons usually being between two and four hours long), enjoy a lunch break and then put your new-found skills into practice in the afternoon, ideally with the people you've been learning alongside – it's surprising how much you can learn from watching colleagues in action.

By taking lessons, you'll develop good techniques right from the start and can follow a programme that will progressively and logically develop your skills. And once you've got beyond the learner stage, lessons are still worth considering – even the best skiers can always pick up something new, and for intermediate skiers, further instruction may be the only way to get off the dreaded intermediate 'plateau'.

SKI CONDITIONS

WEATHER FORECASTS ARE NOW MORE ACCURATE THAN EVER. BUT EVEN SO, MOUNTAIN WEATHER REMAINS NOTORIOUSLY UNPREDICTABLE. WHILST IT PAYS TO LEARN AS MUCH AS YOU CAN ABOUT MOUNTAIN CLIMATES, YOU SHOULD ALWAYS ERR ON THE SIDE OF CAUTION WHEN IT COMES TO THE WEATHER.

READING THE WEATHER

There isn't room here to go into detail on the scientific subject of mountain meteorology, so the best advice is to pay attention to the local weather forecast, which will be available on regional TV stations and radios, the resort's own TV station (many larger resorts have these), and regular bulletins posted in visitor centres, ski shops, lodges and at ski lifts at the base of the mountain. You need to know current and predicted weather conditions including air temperature and snow conditions, both on the mountain and in the immediate area.

Wind and air temperature

There can be a big difference in temperature between the top and bottom of the mountain, and it can go either way. As a rough calculation, air temperatures generally fall by around 1°C per 100 m (328 ft) gain in altitude. However, when the phenomenon known as a temperature inversion occurs (when cold, dense air 'sinks' into valley bottoms and depressions in the landscape), it may be colder at the base of the mountain than on the summit.

Snow crystals go through changes once they have fallen, depending on the air temperature.

Wind reduces the ambient air temperature due to the wind chill effect, by which moving air takes heat away from your body. Wind can make a big difference to how cold it feels – you'll also feel this when you're skiing, and the faster you ski the more pronounced the wind chill will be. The wind chill effect is also very apparent when you're sitting on a chair lift and unable to do anything very physical to keep warm. If there's a wind blowing you'll soon feel the cold, especially if it's also snowing, so consider putting on an extra layer of clothes before you get on the chair in bad weather.

Winds blowing from west to east over a mountain range (the direction from which most snowstorms come), sometimes produce the phenomenon known as the *föhn* wind in the Alps and the *chinook* in the Rockies – these are warm winds that flow down the lee side of a mountain range and can cause severe snow melts. Chinook means 'snow eater' in the local language and this wind has been recorded as raising the temperature by 15°C (59°F) in three minutes.

In Europe, a warm southerly wind coming from the Mediterranean and North Africa can also melt the snow quickly. I've seen entire snow slopes in Europe melt away in little more than 24 hours in such conditions. This can also result in a strange phenomenon where the snow turns a pale orange-yellow colour due to dust being carried aloft from the Sahara desert and deposited on the Alps and Pyrenees.

Snowfalls are not always welcome when you are skiing, as a heavy fall can rapidly reduce visibility, and may also leave you cold and wet.

Snow

Obviously, there has to be bad weather from time to time otherwise there would be no snow on which to ski. It can be great fun to ski when it's actually snowing, but since visibility will be considerably reduced you need to be extra cautious and pay close attention to trail markers and piste maps.

If visibility starts to get very bad, head for slope-side piste markers or trees and ski down alongside them; they help to define the slope and landscape, and you'll find that many experienced skiers choose to ski amongst the trees in bad weather for this very reason. Alternatively, ask if you can tag on behind someone who knows the mountain.

Goggles are vital when skiing in falling snow – it's almost impossible to see where you're going without them, and anti-fog coatings mean that your visibility will not be compromised.

Another thing to consider in poor weather is how the snow conditions may change – thick wet snow (or even rain) falling lower down the mountain may be floating down as nice, light snowflakes higher up due to the lower air temperatures. At the same time, bear in mind that when you ski down into wet falling snow, then get on a chair lift to head back up the mountain, your wet clothes will feel much colder and may even freeze up as you ascend into colder conditions.

Changing conditions can mean imminent danger, so always be aware of what is going on around you when you are in the mountains.

Sun

The sun's rays are more intense at high altitude, making a high factor sunscreen essential when you go skiing. Sunlight reflecting off snow adds to the danger, so remember to put it under your chin, not just on the front of your face.

Dehydration

The combination of intense sunlight, physical activity, altitude and dry mountain air will make you dehydrated, so drink plenty of fluids, but not alcohol, which can dehydrate you even more. If you can keep your urine clear every time you visit the bathroom, then you know you're drinking enough. Common indicators of dehydration are nausea, lethargy, nosebleeds and dry, chapped lips. Recovery is usually quick, and is aided by drinking rehydration salts, such as Dioralyte, or sports drinks.

WEATHER FACTS

• *The most snow to fall in one winter was at Mount Baker in Washington state (USA), where 2,898 cm (1,140 in) fell in the winter of 1998–99.*

• *As a result of a temperature inversion, Miles City (703 m/2,306 ft) in Montana recorded the coldest-ever temperature in mainland USA, at −54°C (−65.2°F).*

• *In the early 1900s, skiers created their own snow terminology including 'fluffy', 'powder' and 'sticky' snow.*

Sunburn is a very real risk on the slopes, so don't forget your sun protection.

SKIN CARE AND SUN PROTECTION

• *Even though it will feel cold, the sun can cause severe burns if you don't protect against it. Windburn is an additional danger. Always carry a good sun cream (SPF 15 or higher depending on your skin type) as well as lip balm, and apply both regularly throughout the day.*

• *It's also vital that you wear good quality sunglasses or goggles to help prevent snow-blindness, an excrutiatingly painful, although not permanent, condition*

• *By the end of the day, your skin will feel dried out due to the dry mountain air, so apply a good quality moisturiser before and after skiing.*

Altitude

At higher resorts (at an altidude of more than 2,400–2,700 m/8,000–9,000 ft) there is also a possibility of altitude sickness. Symptoms include a feeling of general weakness, headaches, nausea, difficulty breathing, dizziness and disturbed sleep. You'll overcome the sleep problem after a day or two acclimatizing, but if any of the other symptoms persist, head back down the mountain and spend a little more time becoming acclimatized. If you feel particularly bad while on the high slopes, the ski patrol can usually help with a small dose of oxygen.

Avalanches

Changes in weather conditions can increase the potential for avalanches – probably the most fearsome risk in the mountains. They are more likely to affect those skiing off-piste, but even so, when you see signs warning of avalanche danger, do the sensible thing and obey them. Incidentally, that deep 'boom!' that may wake you on the morning after a heavy snowfall will almost certainly be the ski patrol setting off explosive charges to disperse snow on potential avalanche slopes.

Avalanches are always a threat, but most novice and intermediate slopes are well out of reach of all but the most severe occurences.

CHOOSING THE RIGHT TRAIL

All resorts grade their slopes by colours which are indicated on piste maps and on the runs. These gradings refer to slopes in ideal conditions – any slope will be harder to ski in poor conditions such as ice, bad light or heavy spring snow. Daily trail reports are posted at the bottom of lifts and in base lodges, hotels or information centres, and should be consulted before you head off onto the mountain. There is a slight variation in the grading colours used in Europe and North America, as indicated in the box below.

Although the gradings are meant to be universal, they are relative to individual resorts. This means that what may be graded green in one place might be the equivalent of blue somewhere else. For example, Sun Valley in Idaho is well known for underestimating trail grades so that most green runs here are the equivalent of a blue at many other resorts.

In all countries, a yellow 'caution' sign warns of poor ski conditions, dangers or obstacles on a trail.

SLOPE GRADINGS			
SLOPE DIFFICULTY	SKIING ABILITY	TRAIL COLOUR	
		EUROPE	NORTH AMERICA
Easy	Beginner	Green	Green
Moderate	Beginner – Intermediate	Blue	Blue
Difficult	Intermediate – Advanced	Red	Black diamond
Most difficult	Advanced – Expert	Black	Double black diamond

READING THE SLOPE

Trail or piste maps will provide you with a good indication of which slopes you'll feel comfortable skiing, but you also need to consider variables such as snow conditions, weather and visibility, objects on the trail and how busy the slopes are.

Much of this can be assessed from the ski lift on the way up the mountain, especially if it follows the line of the trail you intend to ski. Be sure to take a good look at the trails below you as well as at the scenery while you're riding uphill, and your run will be much more enjoyable. Also remember that the weather conditions may be very different at the top of your run than they were at the bottom.

Many of the considerations involved in reading a slope and skiing safely are covered in the internationally recognized 'Skiers' Responsibility Code' (see page 68).

Taking a good, hard look at a slope before you launch yourself down it is extremely sensible; it could save your leg, or your life!

UNDERSTANDING THE FALL LINE

The 'fall line' is simply the most direct route down a slope – or to put it another way, the path that a snowball would follow if rolling down that slope.

Skiing is 99 per cent about travelling diagonally back and forth across the fall line, which allows you to ski downhill at your own pace. It's not often you spend any amount of time skiing directly down the fall line (known as 'schussing') unless you want to go at speed or are skiing down a very gentle slope.

If you want to stop, you simply cut sharply across the fall line or even turn slightly uphill against gravity.

Skiers travel diagonally across the fall line.

The direct route, or fall line, goes straight down a slope.

Skiers usually move from side to side across the fall line, following the natural contours of the mountain.

TYPES OF SNOW

Snow starts its life in clouds high in the atmosphere as single microscopic ice crystals with usually a speck of dust as the nucleus. These crystals grow into the classic six-sided snowflake by attracting water vapour when the temperature is around −15°C (5°F). At higher temperatures they tend to be long and slender, and if it's colder they are more flat and plate-like.

Once snow crystals have fallen and accumulated they continue to go through changes, depending on the air temperature and the morphology of the crystals within the snow mass. The perfect fluffy powder that makes for ideal skiing will only stay this way so long as air temperatures remain close to or below freezing, and even then some settling and consolidation of the snow pack will occur.

If temperatures rise above freezing melting is likely, leading to heavier, wet snow, whilst if the temperature drops below freezing again after a period of melting a crust will form on the surface. Over time layers of varying density will build up in the snow – where these are poorly bonded and the slope is steep enough, slippage and shearing may occur between the layers resulting in avalanches.

On pisted runs in ski resorts the snow is packed down into a perfect, smooth surface, making it easier to ski. However, the continual passage of skis over these groomed runs both wears away the snow and can pack it down so hard that it becomes icy. This is why the 'piste bashers' are brought out every night, grooming the runs back to perfection for the next day – a good reason to get up bright and early if you want to catch the best snow conditions.

For the purposes of this book, we'll divide snow into five catagories, as follows.

Ski heaven – a perfect powder day.

Powder

The best powder occurs when the snow has a low moisture content, keeping the snowpack light and fluffy. This is most likely to occur at high altitude and in dry, cold climates – the classic location for great powder is Utah, where storm clouds have a lot of the moisture 'sucked out' of them as they move over the Great Salt Lake before then precipitating beautiful, talc-dry snow over the peaks of resorts such as Alta and Brighton. Other good locations for powder snow include interior British Columbia and Alberta in Canada, and higher resorts of the Alps such as Tignes and Verbier.

Hard pack

'Hard pack' is the snow you'll find on pisted runs in ski resorts, formed into lines of 'corduroy' by expensive 'piste bashers' to create perfect, easy-to-ski slopes. The piste bashers will create a firm (rather than hard) surface, which allows your skis to carve through it and perform satisfying turns. Were the snow not packed down like this but left in its natural state it would soon become cut up, heavy, icy or bumpy.

Corn snow

A springtime phenomena, 'corn snow' is coarse, wet granular snow caused by the diurnal cycle of melting and refreezing. More experienced skiers find it great fun to ski when the top layer has melted, usually around mid-morning – by early afternoon the sun will have warmed it too much and it'll be wet and slushy.

Top right: 'Corduroy' snow is packed into neat lines by grooming machines.
Right: Head for the edge of the pistes underneath the lifts to find ungroomed snow.

Artificial snow

Many resorts have snowmaking machines, which essentially blast out a fine spray of water which, in sub-zero temperatures, turns to a granular 'snow'. It's not as good to ski on as the real thing, but it's generally acceptable for most skiers and a lot better than rocks and grass.

However, the process is very energy intensive, uses lots of water and requires rather unsightly and noisy snowmaking machines to be set up all over the mountain. It's also often necessary to build reservoirs to store water for use in the machines, so the whole process has a big and somewhat negative impact on the overall mountain environment.

Ice

Icy conditions occur when the temperature rises above freezing, melting the snow, then falls below freezing again (usually at night) to leave a hard, frozen surface. The best way to deal with ice is to keep your ski edges as sharp as possible in the hope that they will cut through it on turns. You should be able to get your edges sharpened at rental/equipment shops in any resort.

TYPES OF SKI LIFTS

Most ski resorts will use a combination of the following types of ski lifts to get you up their mountains. See pages 64–67 for more about using them.

Magic carpet This is essentially the kind of moving walkway you see in airports, which carries you a short distance up the slope whilst standing on your skis. They're used almost exclusively on complete beginner slopes.

Handle tow A handle tow is a cable with a series of handles attached, which you grab hold of to be pulled upslope on your skis. Some more basic ones may not have handles, you just hold onto the cable. As with magic carpets these are used almost exclusively to access short beginner slopes.

T-bars An infernal contraption consisting of an upside down 'T' which is connected by a retractable line to a cable that drags you up the slope. You place the left or right side of the T behind the top of your legs, riding up either singly or with someone else on the other side. Don't sit down on the T or you will end up on the floor.

Button or Poma lift This lift is based on the same principle as the T-bar but instead you have a Frisbee-sized disk attached to a long pole, the pole going between your legs and the disk behind your backside and the whole contraption dragging you up the mountain. It's also sometimes called a 'Poma' after the manufacturer. They are a little easier than T-bars, but either are hard on the legs if it's a long ascent.

Ski lifts get you onto the mountain, so learn to use them with confidence.

Chairlifts These may vary from older one or two-person lifts to state-of-the-art four or six person 'detachable' chairs. This means that the mechanism attaching the chair to the main cable detaches at the top and bottom of the lift, which allows it to move more slowly, making it easier to get on and off. Most also have pull-down safety bars to prevent you falling off, and these also come with footrests which take the strain off your legs. Some also have a pull-down Plexiglass cover for bad weather.

'Bubble' lift A small enclosed cabin, like a mini cable car, which will take around six to eight people. You put your skis in racks on the outside.

Cable cars Cable cars often follow spectacular routes up the mountain, good examples of which are the 3,220 m/10,456 ft) Aiguille Rouges at Les Arcs and the 3,398 m/11,150 ft Lone Mountain Tram at Big Sky, Montana. They may take a hundred or more passengers, in which case it can be a very tight squeeze – try if you can to get to the front of the queue, so you can at least get a spot with a view.

Funicular This is essentially a train up the mountain, often travelling up slopes so steep that the carriages are 'stepped' otherwise the floors would be too steep to stand on. Many, such as those at Tignes, Val d'Isère and Davos go through long, dark tunnels through the mountain, whilst the lovely old funicular that runs half way up the Eiger from the the Swiss resort of Grindelwald is an absolute delight to travel on, even if you don't ski.

Funicular railways are an enjoyable way to gain height on a mountain.

TECHNIQUES

SKIING FOCUSES LARGELY ON TECHNIQUE, AND IT'S WORTH GETTING IT RIGHT BECAUSE BETTER TECHNIQUE NOT ONLY MEANS BETTER SKIING, BUT OPENS UP MORE OF THE MOUNTAIN TO YOU. HOWEVER, AT THE END OF THE DAY, ENJOYING YOURSELF IS WHAT REALLY MATTERS.

PUTTING ON SKIS

Putting on a pair of skis is simple once you have your bindings set up correctly (see page 27). Simply put the toe of your ski boot into the front of the binding, lower your heel, and when you feel the resistance of the binding's heel-piece, push down hard and you'll feel your boot snap into place. This is called clipping in.

If the heel of the binding is in the closed position you won't be able to click into it. To open it, use the end of your pole or your other boot to push down on the tab on top of the binding and, once it's open, clip in.

You need to be on a flat surface when you clip into your skis, or have the skis facing across the slope, otherwise they'll slide away from you. Also, knock any snow off the bottom of your boots before you clip in, since a build up of snow will prevent you from getting the bindings on.

Use your ski poles for balance whilst clipping in, and note that there's usually no 'left' or 'right' in a pair of skis so it doesn't matter which one you put on either foot.

HOLDING YOUR POLES CORRECTLY

Ski poles are essential for balance both whilst skiing and to assist with moving around flatter areas. As you improve you'll find them vital for more technical skiing, too.

Holding your poles correctly is a simple matter. Slide your hand through the pole straps from the bottom and fold your hand around the grip. Keep the straps reasonably loose so you can get your gloved hand in and out easily.

Most people automatically hold the poles in something approximating the correct position, which is with your upper arms at your side and your lower arms bent at around 90 degrees out in front of you. This is the basic position when stationary. However, since you'll be using the poles for balance whilst skiing and to push across the snow on flatter areas, you'll obviously vary this as appropriate, but we'll come to that later.

THE BASIC STANCE

The 'basic stance' in skiing comes naturally to most people as soon as they're clipped into their skis. This is largely because, in order to be comfortable in a pair of ski boots, you have to get your legs into what is essentially the basic stance: your feet facing straight ahead, ankles flexed, knees slightly bent and legs slightly apart in a 'balanced' position. You don't want to feel your calves leaning back against your boots. Instead, your shins should be exerting light but comfortable pressure on the front of the boots and your feet should feel comfortable – don't bunch up your toes or tense your feet in any other way.

Hold your arms out slightly in front of you, with shoulders facing forwards, as if firing a pair of six shooters, which again is a balanced position so will come fairly naturally. Keep your torso as loose and flexible as possible.

This may sound like a lot to remember, but it isn't really – don't forget that you've been balancing on all sorts of surfaces since you were a toddler, and most of the time managing to stay upright quite successfully. Skiing isn't that much harder, and the balanced position is a relatively natural one – all that makes it tricky is that you're sliding downhill on skis at the same time. Don't forget that the original skiers were all self-taught on far more basic equipment than you'll be using; there is really no great mystique to the sport.

Practise the basic stance in your ski boots on the snow before you put on your skis. You can even practise it, with and without ski boots, in the comfort of your own home, hotel or chalet.

Holding your poles correctly

The basic stance

MOVING ON SNOW

Before you start heading down any hills you need to adapt to the weight of the skis, boots and bindings on your feet, as well as get accustomed to the sensation of being on a slippery surface.

To start getting a feel for moving on skis, slide your feet back and forth, lift your skis up and move both forwards and sideways, and walk by sliding your left and right foot forwards alternately. It may feel strange at first, but watch expert skiers and you'll see they're always moving around on their skis – they rarely keep still, even when standing around talking, or studying a piste map.

Personally I feel that it's almost a psychological thing, reminding themselves through feel that they're in total control of their skis as well as constantly retaining the satisfying sensation of co-ordination between skis, boots, feet, legs and upper body. Quite simply, the more you move around on your skis, the more quickly you'll develop an intuitive feel for them.

As you get used to the feel of your skis and boots you'll also find you more readily move into something approximating a 'basic stance', or balanced position. This is all very well on a flat surface, but skiing is about moving downhill.

To stay balanced on skis when you're moving, you'll naturally feel as if you want to spread your stance to widen the base of your support. At the same time, you should open your arms a bit wider, much like a tightrope walker seeking balance.

Find some flat ground and practise getting into this slightly wider, more balanced position; then point the toes on your left foot slightly inwards and the heel out; and repeat with your right foot. You now have the edges on the inside of your skis (not illogically known as the 'inside edges') digging into the snow and putting most, if not all, of the ski's pressure onto the snow's surface. You'll

be standing in a version of the classic snowplough position (see page 58) which, were you moving downhill, would allow you to control your speed by increasing or decreasing the pressure you exert on the ski's edges (the more pressure you exert the slower you go, as we shall see on the following pages).

The next step is to find a gentle slope to ski down, so your recent experience of moving around and walking on your skis will come in useful now. Make sure the slope is gentle enough that you can come to a natural halt at the bottom of it.

Having walked across the flat terrain to the base of a short, gentle incline, turn sideways to the fall line and sidestep up it, as if you were walking sideways up a set of stairs. Angle each ski towards the slope by pushing your knees into the slope a little, and you'll feel and see the ski's edges bite into the snow to stop you slipping.

Practice putting different amounts of pressure on the ski's edges to see just how much (or how little) pressure is required to make your skis bite into the snow and hold you steady.

Once you've made your way 20 m (66 ft) or so up the slope it is time for your first run. Stop, keep your skis facing across the slope (or fall line), turn your upper body to face downhill and at the same time plant your poles into the snow downslope as far as you can, bracing your arms to support yourself.

Now gradually ease both your skis around in small steps until they are also facing downslope, using your poles as brakes to stop you from moving. This is tricky at first, but bear with it!

When you're facing directly downhill, get your skis into the 'basic stance' position with the inside edges biting into the snow, the tips pointing in slightly but remaining apart, and the tails pointing slightly out. When you feel balanced and confident, lift your poles out of the snow and slide slowly downhill. Don't forget to hold your arms out and slightly forwards for additional balance.

In this 'basic stance' position you should glide down this gentle slope, hopefully without falling over, and eventually come to a halt on the flats below. Although it is hard work to start with, repeat this manoeuvre several times until you begin to feel comfortable with the initially uneasy sensation of sliding downhill on skis.

Moving on skis for the first time can be a little daunting, but once you have learned the basic stance and found your balance, you'll soon get the hang of it.

USING YOUR SKIS AS BRAKES

The metal edges of skis are very effective brakes and easy to use – downhill racers slow from 120 kph (75 mph) to zero in the space of 50 m (164 ft) or so at the end of a race. You won't be going anything like that fast, so your skis will slow you even more quickly. Once you can readily stop yourself on skis, your confidence will inevitably increase considerably.

On one of your short downhill runs, try exerting more pressure on the inside edges of your skis by pushing out with your heels and you'll find you slow down, maybe even stop if it's a very gentle incline.

This is because the edges of the ski are scraping against the snow and the friction they exert naturally slows you down – and the more pressure you exert on the edges the slower you go. What you're doing is creating a 'snowplough', a well-known technique for controlling skis (see page 58).

At first, you may find it difficult to put equal pressure on both the left and right ski, and this can result in one ski moving more slowly than the other which will lead to the ski tips crossing and the inevitable fall. Don't worry, it's all part of the learning process and it will take very little time and practice for you to overcome this.

In a classic snowplough turn, the tips of the skis are angled inwards and the back ends point outwards, forming an inverted 'V' shape, with more weight applied to the inside of the turning ski.

THE SNOWPLOUGH TURN

The snowplough (or wedge, as it's often known in North America) is generally regarded as a somewhat inelegant beginners' technique, but that's not entirely true. While it is a beginners' technique (which you should progress beyond within a few hours on skis), and it certainly isn't as elegant as a nice carved turn with parallel skis, a snowplough is not used exclusively by beginners. It is an invaluable technique for controlling your speed, as well as for turning, especially in confined spaces, and all experienced skiers use it several times a day.

You've been doing a basic snowplough already as you were gliding straight down the hill, but you can also use the snowplough to turn. As you glide down your gentle beginner's slope, push down with more pressure on the inside of your right ski (or left, it doesn't really matter). As you push down on your right ski you'll start to veer to the left, the direction in which the tip of your right ski is facing. Do the same with your left ski and you'll veer right. Ease off the pressure on the inside of either ski and the angle of your turn will lessen. All you need to do in order to turn is put more pressure on the inside of one ski or the other and the skis will do the rest for you. And you'll be pleased to know that holds true for virtually all levels of skiing.

If you practice your snowplough technique, you'll find that you can use it to enjoy little journeys of discovery across slopes you were previously just going straight down, so experiment with traverses from one side of the slope to the other, applying different amounts of pressure on the ski you're turning to develop a feel for how much effort is required to perform turns of greater or lesser angles.

Increase pressure on the inside ski to turn.

Sidestepping is one way of getting up a slope on skis. A faster, if more strenuous, method is the herringbone technique.

• Face up the slope, with the tips of your skis pointing out and the tails pointing in, and the edges angled into the snow to prevent you slipping (think of it as being something like the reverse of a snowplough).
• Now simply slide each foot forward alternately as you move up the slope – you may slip back slightly, but you can prevent this by increasing the pressure on the inside of your skis.
• As you get better at the herringbone technique, you can make it more effective by lifting each foot and sliding it forward in the style of an ice skater. You can also use this as a very effective means of moving across flat or gently inclined surfaces.

Use the herringbone technique (see box) to help you get up a slope.

FALLING

Falling is an unavoidable part of skiing. It may sound a bit macho to say that if you don't fall you're not trying hard enough, but there is a certain amount of truth to that – the more you push yourself, the more likely you are to take a tumble or two. As a beginner, you may end up with a few bruises and knocks, but on the whole, snow is a fairly soft material to fall onto, and you won't be skiing very fast while you're learning the basics.

Falling is more likely to bruise your ego than your body, which is why it is good to learn with skiers of the same ability since the chances are, if you fall, so will someone else, which acts as reassurance that you're not that bad after all! It's also a lot easier to laugh about your falls when others are taking tumbles too.

On the slopes you'll be skiing down initially, you'll stop pretty much where you fall, but once you progress to steeper slopes you may slide some distance. You can halt the slide by digging the edges of your skis into the slope, although there is a risk that this may pop a binding.

You only need unfasten the rear binding to 'unclip' from your skis. Most bindings have a small depression on them into which you can push the end of your ski pole, which, if enough pressure is applied, will cause the binding to release.

An alternative way to do this requires a little more balance: move one ski back until your instep is level with the rear binding of the opposite ski, then shift it over the binding, pressing down with the inside edge to release it. Once one foot is free, you can use the free foot to pop open the other binding.

Avoiding injury

Using common sense and standard self-preservation techniques are the best ways to avoid ski injuries. Read the 'Skiers' Responsibility Code' (see page 68) for standard advice on how to avoid hurting yourself and others on the slopes.

Some basic guidelines include:

- Learning to use the ski lifts properly. Don't wait around at the top of a lift in the unloading area, because someone getting off the lift could collide with you. See pages 64–67 for more on using lifts.
- Making sure your bindings are on the correct setting.
- Monitoring your wellbeing. If you feel tired and/or cold, stop for the day. You are far more likely to have an accident when you are not feeling at your best.
- Taking extra precautions in bad light.
- Being aware that not all objects and hazards on the slopes may be marked.
- If you feel you've taken on more than you can handle with a hard run, look for an easy way off the mountain; there will probably be one. As a last resort you can always walk down, but be aware of other skiers coming down the slope and keep to the side of the trail. Of course, you should learn to read a piste/trail map so that you don't end up on slopes you can't deal with.

You can often tell when a fall is about to happen, so try to relax and go with it – that way you're less likely to hurt yourself.

CARRYING SKIS

Skis are quite heavy things, so it's worth learning how to carry them properly to minimize the effort involved. Stand your skis on their tails, and place the ski bases together. The binding brakes will snag onto each other, holding the skis loosely in place. Then lift them up and place them over your shoulder, tips forward and the front of the binding behind your shoulder, balancing them with your hand.

When walking around it is easier, and more comfortable, to unclip the buckles on your ski boots – although they're still pretty unwieldy, so be extra careful on stairs and slippery surfaces such as wooden floors and, of course, ice.

When you are carrying skis in a crowd, don't forget that you have almost 2 m (6.6 ft) of heavy gear with sharp edges over your shoulder. Be aware of other people and where they are in relation to you. Being whacked on the side of the head by someone else's ski is not a pleasant experience!

TIPS FOR BETTER SKIING

You'll undoubtedly feel awkward on skis at first, which is perfectly natural. The best way to get over this is to use your skis as much as possible – it makes sense that the more you ski the better you ski.

- Don't 'force' your snowploughs too much, or have the skis too far apart. It is physically tiring and not that effective.
- Use your poles for balance as well as for support.
- If you start to feel tired or frustrated, stop, or at least take a break. Your skiing will only improve when you're feeling fresh and enthusiastic.
- Ensure all your pockets are zipped up, all the time – you don't want them getting full of snow when you fall. Keys, phones, cash, lift pass and so on should always be kept in a zipped pocket.

Carry your skis over one shoulder, and always be aware of people behind you.

Getting up from a fall

Once you're splayed out in the snow you obviously need to get back up on your skis, which isn't always as easy as it sounds. The best way to do it is as follows.

• Angle both skis across the slope with your backside on the uphill side of them (A).
• Plant both poles in the snow on the uphill side of your skis and push yourself up on them (B) until you are back on your feet (C).
• Keep the edges of your skis weighted into the slope so you don't slip.

   If this proves too difficult or your skis get inextricably caught under your body, just unclip from your bindings (see page 61), take off one or both skis, get up and clip back into your bindings
   Once on your feet you may want to remove wayward snow from inside your clothes − you'll soon know it's there once it starts working its way down the back of your ski pants!

Getting up from a fall is simple when you know how.

USING LIFTS

For many beginner skiers, using ski lifts for the first time can be as daunting as actually skiing down the mountain, but after a while you'll hop on and off them almost without thinking.

On most lifts you'll have to pass through a ticket barrier before you can get on the lift. This can vary from a lift operator checking lift tickets to more high tech devices which will either read your ticket like an ATM (where you stick the ticket in a small slot) or scanning devices which can read the ticket whilst it is in the chest or sleeve pocket of your ski jacket.

For the ATM-type machines your ticket needs to be easily accessible, ideally on a length of elastic around your neck, or on specially made widgets, which you can buy for a very small fee, which attach securely to your jacket at one end and hold the ticket (again, securely) on a retractable elastic line at the other so it can be easily pushed in and out of the machine.

Magic carpet Shuffle up to the 'carpet' on the snow and once the centre of your skis (i.e. your feet) is over the moving section, the lift will smoothly gather you up and move you along at a gentle pace. You may feel yourself pushed slightly backwards by the momentum of the lift when you first start moving so be wary of that. When you come to the end of the lift you should simply ski off onto the snow, but again be wary of your pace changing and throwing you off balance as you hit the snow.

Handle tow Since you have to grab this with one hand, you'll need to hold both ski poles in the other hand. Stand alongside the tow and grab the handle (or rope if it's a rope tow) and be prepared for a sharp jerk forwards as you set off. If you ski

Magic carpet lifts (top) and handle tows (above) are usually very easy to use.

slowly up to one of these lifts you can avoid this 'jerk' to an extent since you'll already have some momentum as you set off. Try to avoid having your arm stretched out full length in front of you as it is a strain, and you'll have less balance on your skis – if you can, keep the handle as close to your body as possible. At the top of the tow simply let go of the handle and use your momentum to ski away from the lift.

T-bar Ski to the bottom of the lift with a partner and stand side-by-side at the 'depart point' (the lift operator will tell you where to stand if you're not sure). Put both your ski poles in the hand which will

T-bar lifts can be tricky, but practise makes perfect.

LIFT ETIQUETTE AND TIPS

• If you're not sure how to use a lift, check the instructions at the bottom of the lift and/or ask the lift operator for assistance.

• On drag lifts, be prepared for a sharp jerk when you set off– balance is everything!

• Try to avoid getting on a T-bar with a child, as they'll need to have the bar much lower than you, so you'll have to go all the way up the slope in a squatting position or with the T-bar behind your calves.

• If you find yourself falling off a drag lift, just let the lift go and ski back down to start again – you're unlikely to hold on all the way to the top and if you do the lift operator will not be happy. Your skis will probably have come off half way up the slope anyway.

• When getting on lifts, especially drags, try not to have the pointy end of your ski poles waving around in the air – you could have someone's eye out.

• Treat lift operators ('lifties') with consideration – it's a thankless and often cold job.

• Don't hang around in the lift queue, or at the top of the lift where you'll just be getting in everyone's way and may cause a collision.

• Keep an eye on where you put your skis in a busy lift queue – people don't always take too kindly to having their skis stomped on by another skier as not only can it scratch them, it means they can't move.

• Look after your lift ticket and keep a record of its details (you can often put these on a detachable strip on the bottom of the ticket when you purchase it). This is the only chance you'll have of getting a replacement should you lose it.

be on the outside of the lift. The lift operator will be just behind you and will place the T-bar just below your backsides with the shaft of the T-bar rising up between the pair of you. Each of you should grab hold of this.

Never sit down on a T-bar. Wait until the cable running from the top of the T-bar's shaft has fully extended (this is attached to the lift cable which pulls the bar up the hill) and it will then take your weight and pull you up the hill on your skis. You often get a bit of a jerky start – watch out for this or it may throw you off balance. Try to keep your skis parallel – if you snowplough you'll push your partners skis from under them. Also try to let your legs relax as much as possible, although this isn't easy.

At the top of the lift you'll have to decide who is getting off first. That person should ski off to the side of the lift, whilst the person getting off last holds on to the T-bar until their partner has safely glided away and then pulls the bar from behind and lets go of it so it retracts back up to the lift cable. Make sure it doesn't hit other skiers.

You can ride T-bars singly, but wait until you've had plenty of practice in pairs as it's a little harder this way and requires more dexterity on skis.

Button/Poma As with a T-bar, ski to the bottom of the lift, place your ski poles in one hand and wait for the lift operator, who will be behind you, to hand you the button. It will be passed to you round the

Chairlifts can be a great opportunity to relax and chat with friends.

side of your left or right shoulder depending on the orientation of the lift, and you should grab a hold of the shaft and place the lower part of it between your legs so your bottom is resting on the 'button' at the base of the shaft. Don't sit down on it!

As with a T-bar, wait for the cable running from the top of the button's shaft to be taken up and then you'll be pulled up the slope – the start can sometimes be abrupt so watch out for this in case it throws you off balance. In some resorts you grab the button yourself from a row of waiting buttons and place it between your legs as described above. It will set off automatically once you have hold of it.

Keep your skis parallel as you glide uphill and try to relax your legs and your grip on the shaft. At the top of the lift you'll need to pull the button down and out from between your legs, let go of it and use your momentum to ski off to one side. Watch out for other skiers when letting go of the button.

Chairlifts Things get considerably more relaxing with chairlifts, since you're sitting down rather than 'skiing' all the way to the top of the run. You'll shuffle up to the bottom of the lift on your skis, and the lift operator will ensure that you and your fellow riders (chairs can hold from one to eight people) are standing in a lie abreast, ready to get on the chair.

Hold your poles in one hand and look over your shoulder as the chair approaches. If it's a 'detachable' chair it will move towards you very slowly and as you feel it nudge your calves just sit down on it. Non-detachable chairs will be 'handed' to you by the lift operator to ensure they don't hit you in the back of the legs.

Once you're sitting on the chair, keep your ski tips up so they don't catch on the ground beneath, and once everyone is settled in you should reach up and pull down the safety bar, which will probably also have footrests attached. At the top of the

Bubble lifts offer great views of the resort.

lift you'll need to raise the bar (watch out for signs on the lift stanchions advising when to do so), lift your ski tips again, and as the base of your skis touch the ground, stand up and let the momentum of the lift allow you to ski off. Move quickly away from the departure area so you don't get in the way of skiers coming up behind you.

Bubble lifts, cable cars and funiculars You have to remove your skis to ride all these lifts, and you simply walk into the lift, get as comfortable as you can (seats are sometimes available) and try to get close to a window to enjoy the view.

At the top you just walk out and onto the snow where you clip back into your skis. Note that on bubble lifts you may have to place your skis in a rack on the outside of the lift.

AVOIDING COLLISIONS

In a busy ski resort there may be thousands of people moving down, across and maybe even up the slopes at various speeds and with various levels of skill, so collisions are a distinct possibility.

Collisions can be serious – two average intermediate skiers heading hell for leather down a red run are likely to be travelling at up to 55 kph (35 mph) each. If they crash into each other, the potential for injury is high. Indeed, people have been killed and seriously injured as a result of collisions with fellow skiers and boarders, so it pays to be aware of what other skiers are doing around you.

The Skiers' Responsibility Code (see below) provides great advice for staying safe on the piste, and bear in mind that just because you're out in the wild blue yonder it doesn't necessarily mean someone won't be keeping an eye on the slopes to ensure they remain as safe as possible. Ski patrollers have the authority to confiscate lift tickets from skiers they deem to be skiing dangerously (in some US resorts they may even have radar guns to check your speed) and you can even be prosecuted by the police if it's considered that you're responsible for a serious skiing accident.

Right: Changes in the weather can be sudden – make sure you are prepared.
Below: Always be aware of skiers around you.

SKIERS' RESPONSIBILITY CODE

- *Always stay in control and be able to stop or avoid other people or objects.*
- *People ahead of you have the right of way. It is your responsibility to avoid them.*
- *Do not stop where you obstruct a trail or are not visible from above.*
- *Whenever starting downhill or merging into a trail, look uphill and yield to others.*
- *Always use devices (such as straps) to help prevent runaway equipment.*
- *Observe all posted signs and warnings. Always keep off closed trails and out of closed areas.*
- *Prior to using any lift, you must have the knowledge and ability to load, ride and unload safely.*

In the mountains the weather can change very rapidly so you need to be able to adapt equally rapidly to these changes. Here are a few ways of doing so:

• Ensure you have spare clothing in case the weather turns bad (or that you have easy access to it, for example at the resort's base lodge). If you ski with a rucksack you can carry a spare base layer/mid layer, spare inner gloves, a scarf etc. And if the weather turns warm it means you can take off a layer or two.

• Always carry goggles. You may prefer to ski in sunglasses, but if it starts to snow goggles are far more effective.

• If you start to feel cold, get inside and get warm as soon as possible.

• If weather conditions become so bad that you are enduring rather than enjoying your skiing, call it a day. You're here to have fun, after all, and in bad weather there's far more chance of hurting yourself in a fall or collision than in good weather.

BUILDING SKILLS

ONCE YOU'VE MASTERED THE BASICS, YOUR WHOLE SKI CAREER WILL BE ABOUT DEVELOPING YOUR SKILLS SO YOU CAN SKI MORE OF THE MOUNTAIN IN MORE STYLE. BUT TRY NOT TO GET TOO SERIOUS ABOUT IT – SKIING IS ABOUT FUN, AFTER ALL.

THE PHYSICS OF SKIING

You shouldn't expect to have equations drifting through your head as you ski down a slope, but understanding the basic science behind how a ski works can definitely help you to ski better.

Modern sidecut skis are designed to do most of the work for you, especially turning, which is what skiing is all about. Think about it – the only time you ever really see skiers going straight down a mountain is in ski races. Recreational skiers of all abilities spend the whole day turning their skis across the fall line. This is both the challenge and the joy of the sport.

A huge amount of research and development and hi-tech materials go into the manufacture of skis that will turn effectively. However, what it all comes down to is that your skis can perform two types of turn – a 'skidded' turn and a 'carving' turn.

Both of these turns occur as a direct result of the shape of the ski; you'll notice how the tips are the widest point, coming in to the narrowest point (the 'waist') beneath your feet, then opening out again at the tail. This elongated hourglass shape is the sidecut of the ski, and is what gives it so much turning ability.

INSIDE-OUTSIDE/UPHILL-DOWNHILL

From now on we'll use the terms 'inside' and 'outside' ski when describing the actions your skis are performing. These are terms used universally amongst skiers and, simply put, when you make a turn the inside ski is the ski on the uphill side of the slope and the outside ski is the one on the downhill side.

The terms 'uphill' and 'downhill' ski also refer to the same thing, with the uphill ski being the same as the inside ski, and the downhill ski being the outside ski

This means that on a right turn it's your right ski that's the inside ski and left ski that's the outside ski, and vice versa for a left turn.

Most crucially, all turns in skiing are made using the outside ski.

TURNS

Skidded turns

In a skidded turn, the wide tip of the ski skids or brushes across the snow more deeply than the rear of the ski and meets resistance from the snow, causing the tail of the ski to 'skid' out behind it. The ski will still be moving forward at the same time as it's skidding, leaving a broad track in the snow behind.

To make a skidded turn you simply pivot the outside ski at an angle to your forward direction, and the ski will then oblige by skidding across the snow – you're already doing this in the snow-plough turns we discussed in chapter four (see page 58–59).

Skidded turns

'Real' turns

'Real' turns usually involve a combination of skidding and carving, to greater or lesser degrees, depending on the skill of the skier, the terrain, the snow quality, etc. This will be apparent if you look at the tracks most good skiers leave behind them, which may start as a skidded turn, become a carved turn then finish off as a skid again.

Although 'carving' is the big deal in modern skiing, there's absolutely nothing wrong with skidded turns and, in many instances, they're more effective than carved turns, for example in mixed snow conditions, or for stopping quickly.

When you're first learning, and doing snow-plough turns, you're essentially doing a very basic skidded turn by putting more pressure on one ski than the other when you want to turn. The outside/downhill ski does the work (with a little help from you) with the inside/uphill ski doing very little other than following the outside ski. It is this principal that leads us on to the next step in skiing which is the 'christie' turn.

Carved turns

Christie turns

Christie turns are named after Christiania (now Oslo) in Norway, where the turn was invented a couple of centuries ago. A christie is basically a turn that ends with both skis parallel to one another and it can be achieved by most skiers soon after learning to do a snowplough turn because it follows on the snowplough movements.

When you make a snowplough turn your inside ski isn't really doing much. If it's doing anything at all it's slightly resisting the turn you're making. Think about it – you put your weight onto your left ski in order to turn right, which means you automatically take some weight off your right ski, which then drifts across the surface of the snow whilst the left ski performs the turn for you.

Do that turn again and let it go right through to its logical conclusion, which will have you facing across the fall line and coming to a halt. This time try to consciously take all the weight off your inside ski. This will not only reduce the strain on your uphill foot, ankle and leg, but even better, it should allow the inside ski to follow the outside ski around the arc of the turn in a more or less parallel fashion, and certainly by the time you finish the turn both skis should be close to parallel.

All that's required to move from making snowplough turns to parallel turns is practice and a little thought. As you head into a snowplough turn think about that loose, 'floating' inside ski. Instead of letting it just hang around vaguely following the route of your outside ski in a the classic 'V' shape of a snowplough turn, try to lift it so it just brushes the surface of the snow and at the same time follows the path of your outside ski.

This will make both skis more or less parallel almost from the start of the turn, with the weighted outside ski leading the unweighted inside ski around the arc of the turn to produce a skidded parallel turn. Practise, practise, practise and you'll be surprised how quickly you can progress from snowplough turns to more effective, and far more stylish, christie turns.

The hardest part of making the progression to christie-style turns is usually the transition between turns, and you may find that you go back into snowplough position at this point, or perform a rather jerky 'twist' of the skis into the new direction you want to go.

In order to overcome this, it often helps to have a bit of speed as you go into the transition. Try to focus on making the whole sequence one smooth motion with one ski following the line of the other – this smooth, flowing style is at the very heart of skiing well and stylishly.

CHRISTIE TIPS

• *Try to maintain your speed through each of the turns.*

• *'Unweight' the inside ski.*

• *Allow the inside ski to follow the arc of the outside ski.*

• *Try to keep your turns as smooth and flowing as possible – the whole sequence should be one smooth movement.*

Christie turn

SCHUSSING

'Schussing' is a German word for skiing straight down the fall line. It's what most non-skiers consider the sport to be all about. However, after just a few minutes on skis you'll realize that skiing is all about turning across the fall line, controlling your speed and stopping as and when necessary, rather than hurtling downhill in a straight line.

However, there are times when you'll need, even want, to schuss. The obvious example is when you're skiing down a very gentle incline and need to maintain speed; here, going in a straight line is far more effective as a means of maintaining your momentum. There are also times when you'll want to go straight down the fall line as fast as possible just for the joy of it – after all, skiing is first and foremost about having fun.

By keeping your weight evenly balanced over both skis, with both the tips facing forward (or with a slight 'V' when you're at the beginner stage) you can maintain a straight line down the slope. With your weight spread evenly on both feet, flex your ankles, lean your shins against your boots, bend your knees and keep your upper legs flexed. Your body should face down the hill and your arms should be held out for balance as in the 'basic stance' position (see page 54).

Once you feel confident on your skis and can easily keep them both in a straight line without the tips pointing inwards, try putting a little weight on the inside edge of first one ski, then the next. Not enough to perform a turn, but enough to bite a little way into the snow. This allows you to go faster, as less of the base of the ski is moving across the snow and, although it will cause you to veer left or right at a gentle angle, you'll be able to maintain a fairly straight line by making small weight adjustments on either foot.

Schussing fast through untracked powder.

The other advantage of using your edges like this is that you're less likely to 'catch an edge'. When the bases of your skis are moving flat on the snow it's not uncommon for one of the edges to 'catch' on small undulations such as tracks gouged by other skiers or snowcats etc. and these can knock you off balance.

If you watch experienced skiers on gentle inclines, you'll see that they often 'weight' one ski and then the other to cut long, wide angles across the slope – it's not schussing in the true sense, but it's an effective way to get down the slope in total control. It also provides useful practice at weighting your skis.

TRAVERSING AND SIDESLIPPING

There's some crossover between traversing and sideslipping, although both are distinct actions. Traversing is the process of skiing from one side of a slope to the other without turning, which may or may not involve some sideslipping; while sideslipping is sliding (as opposed to skiing) down the slope and is particularly useful on steep inclines when you can't or don't wish to ski down the slope – you can sideslip down instead. It's also very useful for just manoeuvring around on your skis.

To traverse: put all your weight on the downhill ski, using your foot to push the inside edge of the ski into the snow. Your extended downhill leg takes the strain of the traverse. The uphill ski should be merely skimming across the surface and not directing your course in any way; its tip should also be slightly ahead of the downhill ski. This should come quite naturally as it is a more natural stance when traversing than having both skis parallel. It also prevents the tips crossing and the inevitable fall that would result.

Sideslipping can be useful when you feel out of your depth on a run that's too steep.

Another thing that tends to come naturally is to spread your arms, giving better balance. On steep slopes your uphill pole will catch in the snow so you may need to elevate it slightly. In doing so, the movement of your arm will help to improve your balance.

The essence of traversing is to be totally balanced over the downhill ski.

To sideslip: relax the muscles in your downhill foot and leg and allow the ski's inside edge to slip downslope over the snow's surface rather than bite in, as in a traverse. With the inside edge of the downhill ski unweighted it simply slips down the slope. The uphill ski floats over the surface and follows the downhill ski down the slope, with your arms providing balance, as in traversing.

However, you still need to be balanced over this downhill ski, and perfectly centred over it. If you move your weight forward you'll sideslip down and slightly forwards; move your weight back and you'll sideslip down and slightly backwards.

It helps if you tilt your body slightly downslope as you sideslip, away from the incline of the slope – not an easy thing to do at first, since the natural reaction is to lean into the hill. You don't have to tilt far, so be confident and try it. You'll notice the difference because it effectively places your weight over the centre of the downhill ski, just where it needs to be.

If you want to stop your sideslip, simply increase the pressure on the downhill ski and you'll make the ski's edge bite into the snow and act as a

Traversing

Sideslipping

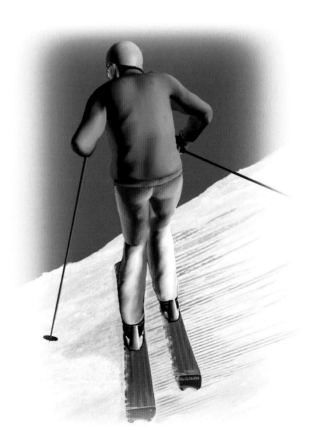

brake. Sideslipping is a practical tool, especially on slopes that you may find too steep to ski confidently. It is also a great way to develop a feel for the inside edges of your skis. By practising sideslipping, you'll discover the nuances of increasing and decreasing the pressure on the inside edge and what effect it has.

SKIING ON ONE SKI

To get a feel for the effectiveness of 'weighting' your skis and the turning qualities of the design, practise skiing on one ski. This is not as hard as it sounds. Find a very gentle slope and as you're schussing, lift one foot ever so slightly off the ground. Skis, boots and bindings are heavy, so you won't be able to lift your foot much and still keep your balance. Change feet and ski on the other leg.

It's important to use your hands and poles to assist your balance, and there's no need to ski very far on one ski. By alternating between the two, you'll further develop your feel for skis and the interplay between them and your feet.

A good tip is to relax your raised leg as much as possible, so that the tip of your ski points down, almost brushing the snow (the base of your ski only needs to be an inch or two above the snow).

Skiing on one ski

Although skiing is all about enjoying the freedom of the mountains, you can't just go tearing around without any consideration for others.

Ski etiquette

- Take time to read the international 'Skiers' Responsibility Code' (see page 68); you'll see reminders on chairlift pylons as well as on your piste map. It covers all the basics for ensuring that everyone has a good day.
- Take your rubbish home, even the biodegradable waste (orange peel, for instance, can take up to five years to rot). After all, it is also the environment that makes for an enjoyable day on the mountain.
- Be polite and patient in lift queues.
- Park considerately – it's difficult enough to negotiate an icy car park in ski boots and carrying skis without finding you've been blocked in when you reach your car.
- Don't drink excessive amounts of alcohol when skiing.

Learning the etiquette of skiing should help to avoid collisions with other skiers.

Always be polite in lift queues and wait your turn with patience.

Once you start covering more ground on the mountain it's inevitable that you'll come across ice, usually as a result of freeze/thaw action and heavy skier traffic. Few people enjoy skiing over ice, but if you look upon it as a challenge and a learning process, rather than something to be feared and avoided, you'll gain more from the experience.

First off, it pays to have sharp edges (good to have in all conditions, but particularly important when encountering ice). That way, if the ice isn't too hard, there's a chance your edges may provide you with some grip.

When you actually hit ice, remain relaxed and don't start forcing your edges in as hard as possible to try and control your turns. It's the equivalent of a car driver slamming on the brakes when he hits an icy patch – all that will happen is you'll go into a skid.

Instead, try to lighten your weight on the skis and 'float' across the ice. If it's just a small patch, this may carry you safely across to the good snow on the other side. If it's a large area of ice you'll probably need to turn at some point. Approach those turns as gently and lightly as possible, using your arms for balance and trying to perform a sliding turn, using the base of the ski rather than the edges. Look out for patches of snow amongst the ice where you may be able to make a better turn.

TIPS FOR IMPROVING YOUR TECHNIQUE

- Most people have a 'stronger' side and so will naturally put weight on their left or right ski, making it easier to do a left or right turn. Becoming equally adept at both is, as with most things, simply a matter of practice.

- Don't be afraid to use a snowplough as a back-up in an emergency or if you feel uncomfortable doing christies on a steeper slope. It's a very effective form of braking and slowing down. If using it helps keep your confidence and enjoyment levels up, then it's got to be a good thing.

- When you hit a flatter, 'boring' stretch of the slope, or maybe a long cat track, practice techniques such as skiing on one ski, traversing and schussing. You can practice sideslipping at the top of a slope whilst waiting for friends to get off the lift or to catch up with you.

- Remember to 'feel your feet' when making a turn. This is the only contact your body has with your skis and your feet tell the skis what to do. Given proper instructions, modern carving skis will do the rest for you.

- Look ahead! You should be keeping a constant eye on what the slope ahead of you is doing so you can adapt to changes in terrain, other skiers crossing your path, etc.

- Listen! When you're heading up on the chair, listen to the sound of the snow under the skiers riding beneath you. The noisier it is, the harder the snow will be and the less fun to ski, and if it's positively clattering then you've got ice. This will tell you which runs you may want to avoid on the way down.

ADVANCED SKILLS

AS YOUR SKILLS DEVELOP FURTHER, MORE OF THE TRAILS ON THE PISTE MAP OPEN UP TO YOU, WHICH EQUALS INCREASED FUN AND EXCITEMENT – AND BETTER VALUE FOR MONEY! COVER AS MUCH GROUND AS YOU CAN, BECAUSE THE MORE YOU SKI THE BETTER YOU'LL GET.

By now you should have learnt the basics of skiing and be ready to move to the next level – that smooth, flowing technique that appears effortless and can be applied on almost any terrain. Unfortunately, the only way to become an accomplished skier is to spend lots of time on the snow practising the correct moves until they become second nature. However, 'practising' your skiing is about as much fun as you can have and is what you do every time you carve down the piste or float through the powder.

Linking your turns is more efficient and instantly makes you look like a pro.

LINKED TURNS

Although by now you should be able to turn on your skis using christies (see pages 74–75) you are probably not yet performing your turns in a swift, flowing movement – each turn will tend to be a discrete action in itself rather than linking sinuously and almost imperceptibly into the next one.

Since skiing is all about turning, it makes sense (as well as being good technique) to be able to link your turns as you progress downslope. Not only is it good practice, it is also more effective, more enjoyable and more stylish skiing.

Let's say you're performing a right-hand christie-style turn across the slope. All your weight is on your left ski and the right ski is unweighted and coming along for the ride, as it should be. To make a smooth transition into your next (i.e. left) turn, you need to place your weight on your uphill ski just before you go into the turn.

This does two things – it prevents you from skidding and twisting the ski as in a christie (the result of your weight on the ski) and at the same time it stops the tail of the downhill ski from skidding out. This produces a decent parallel turn. On top of that, as you go into your next turn your uphill ski's inside edge will bite into the snow and carve rather than skid, whilst your downhill ski, now unweighted, follows it around the turn. All this happens very quickly and your weighted uphill ski very soon becomes your weighted downhill ski as you go into the turn, with your uphill ski again being unweighted and following the downhill ski.

You need a bold approach, since you should also lean your body slightly down the hill as you go into the turn in order to keep your weight over the front of the skis. This will give you better balance on the skis, especially if you keep your arms slightly out to your sides.

The hardest part is probably the brief moment between transferring your weight to the uphill ski and the ski turning and becoming your downhill ski, because at this point your skis are no longer providing the stable base you've got used to in snowploughs and christies.

It takes time and commitment to get to grips with linked turns, and it also helps if you relish that moment of 'lightness' as you move onto the uphill ski, much as you might enjoy the thrill of weightlessness on a roller coaster ride. Added to that you need faith that your skis will respond to your manoeuvre – which they will!

LEANING BACK

In a good balanced stance, your body should lean forward at a slight angle. However, once you get into linked turns it's more important than ever to be aware of the need to keep your weight forward. This is not always easy, especially as you progress onto steeper slopes, because the natural tendency is to lean back due to the understandable fear of falling if you lean downhill.

However, by leaning back you actually increase the chance of taking a tumble, because this forces your skis out in front of you, causing them to move faster across the snow, and almost certainly pushing you off balance. You can end up in a Catch-22 situation here – you lean back a little, your skis pick up speed and your balance is compromised, so you lean back even further, exacerbating the situation until eventually, speeding down the hill, you lose control and wipe out.

As with almost everything in skiing, the only way to overcome your brain and body's natural reluctance to lean down the hill is to practise and be aware that when you're weighted properly on your skis – that is, leaning forward – you always have more control.

Linked turns can be hard at first, but are worth persevering with.

1 Weight is on downhill ski.

2 Transfer weight to uphill ski.

3 Keep weight on downhill ski and extend arms slightly for balance.

4 Begin to transfer weight to uphill ski again.

5 Extend arms slightly and put weight on downhill ski. Uphill ski is unweighted.

ADVANCED CARVING

The basics of carved turns were dealt with in the previous chapter (see page 75), where you discovered that your skis will do most of the work for you if they're given the right instructions by your feet. However, enjoying the exhilarating sensation of high speed carving requires a more dynamic combination of your skis and your body working together, along with a good deal of confidence in the ability of your skis to do what is asked of them.

I was lucky to get a free lesson in carving a few years ago at Sun Peaks in British Columbia from former Olympic downhill gold medallist Nancy Greene, and her advice, which I'm happy to pass on, still holds true today.

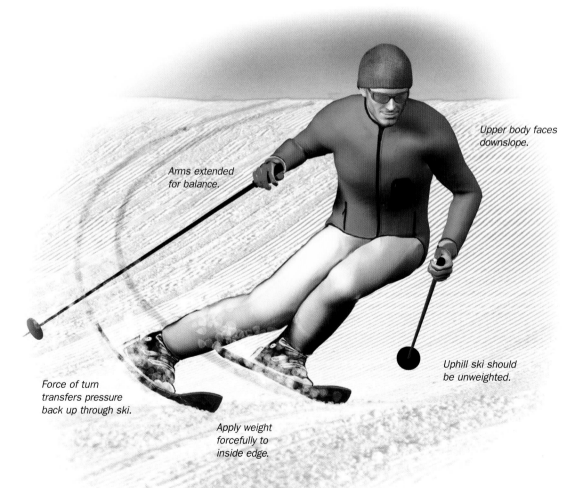

Upper body faces downslope.

Arms extended for balance.

Uphill ski should be unweighted.

Force of turn transfers pressure back up through ski.

Apply weight forcefully to inside edge.

Start off by schussing down a wide, open blue or red run (you don't want the slope to be too gentle). Get up a bit of speed, and then transfer all your weight to one ski and force the inside edge into the snow, making it bite. This will automatically cause the ski to turn, so take the weight off your uphill ski and continue pushing down on the inside edge of your downhill ski with the inside of your foot. If you're going fast enough and pushing hard enough, you should feel the edge of the ski actively cutting into the snow and even transferring pressure back to your foot and up through your leg. Try to keep your upper body facing down the slope and use your downhill (outside leg) to lean into the slope; the uphill leg does very little other than lift the uphill ski so that it glides across the snow. The end result of all this is that you will perform a carved turn, with your skis cutting a sharp, clean arc through the snow.

When you see skilled skiers carving hard it may look as though they're leaning their whole body into the turn, but this is something of an optical illusion. Their momentum, coupled with the angle of their downhill leg, will be such that their upper body inevitably leans a little into the slope, but it is still the legs that are doing most of the turning/leaning.

The harder you turn, the more you'll need to spread out your arms to act as a fulcrum to help you maintain your balance. Don't be afraid to use your arms and poles – that's their job and they're far more effective like this than dangling by your side.

If you allow your outside ski to follow a carved turn through its natural arc you'll find that you end facing uphill to a greater or lesser degree, carried there by the momentum of your turn. It's worth doing this a few times to get a feel for the amazing efficiency of the sidecut and edges in modern skis.

What you should find as you apply pressure at speed when skiing down the mountain is that as

long as you maintain your angle on the ski's edge it will carve into the snow and create a lovely smooth arc. However, this does require a reasonable amount of physical strength, particularly in your thigh, calf and core muscles, the more so the faster and harder you carve.

If you release pressure on a carved turn, your ski's edge will cut less effectively into the snow and may eventually slide out to produce a skidded turn, and that skidding action can be used to perform a hockey stop, one of the easiest and most fun tricks in skiing.

HOCKEY STOPS/ EMERGENCY STOPS

Once you are comfortable with high-speed carving, you can do dramatic and fun 'hockey stops' (named after the way ice hockey players skid to a halt), simply by letting your carving downhill ski slip out into a skidded turn, then pushing hard against the downhill ski's inside edge, as if you were sideslipping.

This will bring you to an abrupt halt, with both skis parallel, and send a satisfying plume of snow flying into the air, ideally all over the friend waiting downslope for you.

However, hard braking like this also has an obvious practical purpose should you need to stop suddenly – such as when you encounter an unexpected obstacle, or if another skier falls in front of you.

SHORT LINKED TURNS

As you progress to skiing steeper slopes you'll find that you need to produce faster, shorter turns, since slower, longer turns will cause you to build up too much speed resulting in difficulty staying in control.

As you go into a turn, control your speed by applying pressure to the outside ski. The edge will bite and slow you down, but you're aiming for a skid

rather than a carve (you rarely, if ever, use carved turns on really steep slopes). As you slow down, you'll feel pressure being exerted back up your legs; use this to unweight and lift upwards, at the same time planting your downhill ski pole and pushing up off this.

As you unweight, you should go into your next turn, pivoting the skis around and allowing the inside edge of your uphill ski to make contact with the snow and move into a light skid turn, which will continue to control your speed.

If you need to slow down more, increase the skid. Your upper body should face downhill as much as possible throughout these turns, with your legs and skis pivoting beneath it. Keep your legs spread slightly, about hip-width apart, as this will provide more stability and balance in the turns.

Apply enough pressure to the outside ski to force it into a skid.

Tail of ski should slide out.

Push off your downhill pole.

MOGUL/BUMP SKIING

Moguls, or bumps, to use the more descriptive word for these lumps of snow, tend to be a 'love them or hate them' thing for most skiers, and the majority fall into the latter camp.

Bumps occur due to the heavy passage of skiers whose regular turns on the same patches of snow eventually push up hard, unforgiving lumps. Unless the slope is groomed, the bumps will remain. Most resorts deliberately leave some areas ungroomed to allow mogul fields to develop. You'll also find bumps in areas that can't be reached by grooming machines, such as underneath lift tower lines.

Since all ski resorts have moguls you might as well learn to ski them; once the challenge has been overcome they can be good fun. You'll also find that once you get moguls mastered you'll often have the slopes on which they occur almost to yourself, since few skiers (and even fewer snowboarders) like to take them on.

Bumps are challenging because they continually throw you off balance. As you ski to the top of a bump you'll be thrown backwards on your skis; you then drop down the other side with an increase in speed and can get thrown even further back, affecting your control. As you hit the trough between bumps, ready to ski up the next one, you may be thrown forwards, reducing your control even further. It's not surprising that skiers of all levels of ability choose to avoid these snowy lumps. The key to getting your skis back under control in a mogul/bump field is: slow down and loosen up.

Find a small, 'unintimidating' bump field to practise on. As you hit the front slope of the first bump, move your weight forwards and allow your legs to absorb the bump; this will prevent you from being thrown back on your skis and will keep your speed under control.

BUMP TIPS
• *Build up gradually, starting on tiny bumps and slowly working towards bigger ones.*
• *Do some exercises to loosen up before you hit the moguls, even if it's only a bit of deep breathing. More than in any other aspect of skiing, your body takes a pounding on a long bump run, so the looser and more relaxed you are, the better it will cope with it.*
• *If you intend to spend any time playing in the bumps, consider using shorter skis, since they are easier to negotiate and turn through the tight little gullies between bumps.*
• *Look ahead and anticipate your run through the mogul field. Think two or three bumps ahead rather than just concentrating on the bump in front of you.*
• *Don't take on a bump run wearing a heavy and/or loose rucksack.*

At the top of the bump, initiate your turn, so that as you drop down the far side of it, your skis are already turning. Here's where it gets tricky, though. Unlike the parallel and carving turns you've been doing so far, where your downhill ski takes all the weight and your uphill ski merely follows it, you need to actively turn both skis at the same time.

The downhill ski still does all the edging and controls the turn, but you need to make sure your uphill ski isn't just flopping around loosely or, worse still, going into a christie-style turn, which will lead to a loss of control and the inevitable fall.

What you should be doing is sideslipping with your downhill ski. This slows you down in a controlled manner as you negotiate the downhill side of the bump. Once you hit the trough of the bump you should be completing your turn, and letting your legs absorb the impact as you slow down on hitting the dip (A). You should still be leaning forwards over the skis, and ready to lean forwards a little more to absorb the next bump as you rise up it.

Note that all the work, both turning and absorbing, is being done by your legs and core muscles, and your upper body should remain facing straight down the hill as much as possible (B). Watch expert bump skiers as they fly down a mogul field; their legs will be pumping rapidly whilst their upper body remains as still as a statue.

Your arms play a vital role in bump skiing. They should be pumping the ski poles, with your downhill arm reaching forwards down the slope to plant the pole and provide you with a fulcrum on which to balance (C).

That word 'balance' is important, because as you ski through bumps you're constantly speeding up and slowing down, absorbing and releasing energy and being thrown backwards and forwards as you ride up and down the bumps. The natural tendency is to tense your muscles, ready for the pounding they're about to get. However, tense muscles don't respond to all these changes efficiently or quickly, so you need to relax as much as possible as you bounce through the bumps. This is easier said than done, but if you can ease the tension in your legs (and mind) and flow into that top turn, you'll find it much easier to negotiate the sideslip down the side and the absorption of the dip of each mogul.

Skiing over/around moguls.

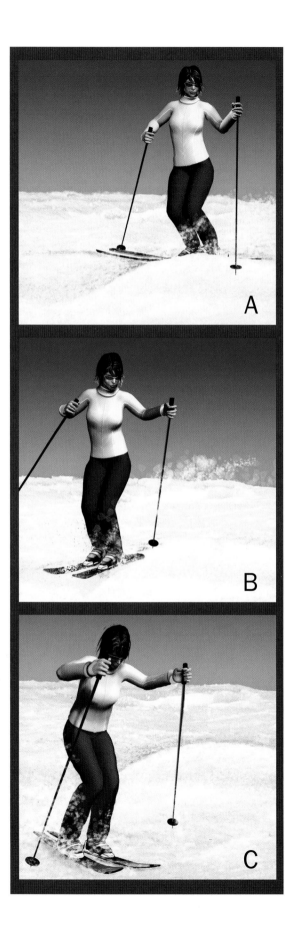

STEEP SKIING

Steep skiing is perhaps the most exciting, but potentially scary, form of skiing; after all, it is not natural to launch yourself headlong down a steep slope. But what is 'steep'?

This, of course, depends on the skill and experience of the individual skier. A beginner will consider a blue or red run to be steep, while an expert skier may get little excitement out of anything less than a black run. But whilst the individual definition of steep will vary, experienced skiers will generally consider most black runs to be 'steep' to some extent, although these can vary within a resort and also from resort to resort.

Steep skiing is exhilarating, but be sure your technique is sound before you try it.

WHAT IS STEEP?

The angles of slopes can be deceptive – watch a ski race on TV and it often seems like the competitors are skiing down relatively flat slopes, but stand alongside that slope in the real world and you'll discover that it's anything but flat.

The same illusion is created when viewing a slope from a ski lift. The only way to get a feel for the incline of a trail is to stand at the top or bottom of it. It's worth ensuring that there's an alternative route if you find yourself at the top of a run that looks too steep for you.

For the record, most black runs are around 20–35 degrees, while serious off-piste steeps will be 30–40 degrees or more. Some extreme skiers will head for slopes in excess of 50–55 degrees, where you really do not want to fall – and if you do, you certainly won't stop any time soon.

The secret of skiing steeps is staying in control, and being confident and relaxed; and if you can cope with short linked turns, then you're part of the way there. This is because you need to perform fast, short, skidded turns in order to keep your speed under control on steep slopes. Long carving turns are no use, as in no time at all you'd be hurtling down the mountain at high speed and out of control. The idea of skidding is that it slows you down and gives you more control, making you and the people around you much safer.

Find a short, steep stretch of snow to practice on – there's no point intimidating yourself by heading for a long, steep run where a fall may mean a long, unstoppable slide. Set off down the hill and immediately go into a skidded short linked turn, at the same time planting your pole firmly downhill in front of you.

Your pole is a vital piece of equipment for steep skiing. Plant it firmly as the skidding action of the outside ski brings you to the slow point of your turn. Use it for support – it will help both the skis and your legs lighten, and you can then hop very slightly up off the snow as you go into your next turn. Keep your heels higher to prevent the tails of the skis catching in the snow and, with your feet and skis now virtually weightless, you will find it much easier to go into the next turn.

Steep skiing

Body is facing downhill.

Body is centred over the skis.

Legs are hip-width apart for stability, strength and balance.

Weight is down aggressively on the downhill ski to produce a skidded turn.

Your upper body should face down the fall line whilst your legs and skis pivot beneath it, and at the end of each turn you can increase your control by jamming your skis' edges into the snow with your feet for extra bite. This will slow you down still further and also provide a rebound of energy back up your legs, which will provide enough momentum to help with the next 'hop'.

You need to keep your weight centred over the skis for full control (leaning back will cause you to lose control and fall) and to remain as relaxed and loose as possible. This sounds very easy on paper but requires a lot of time and commitment to get right.

STEEP TIPS

- *Be prepared to fall, because you will do so at some point (see 'falling', page 60)*
- *When you take on a new and challenging slope, consider starting off by sideslipping into the top of it. This will give you a chance to get a feel for the pitch of the slope, examine its lower reaches and get yourself into a relaxed, balanced stance on your skis.*
- *If the slope gets too steep for you, sideslip down it – it's far safer than risking a bad fall or psyching yourself out.*
- *If a slope is so steep that you may have trouble halting your slide in a fall, ensure there are no rocks, cliffs or other dangerous obstacles in your most likely 'fall line'.*

KICK TURNS

Kick turns are used on very steep terrain where you want to turn on the spot, or in confined spaces (e.g. trees, ridges – even busy lift queues). It requires good leg, thigh and hip flexibility as well as good balance.

To perform a kick turn to the left, for instance, raise your left leg so your ski is vertical to the ground with the tail resting in the snow, then move your leg outwards at the same time as swinging your hips around to the outside of the slope.

The weight of the ski will naturally cause it to pull towards the ground, and it should be facing out and slightly backwards.

You then transfer as much weight as you can on to the left ski, lift your right ski and swing it around, almost as if you were trying to kick a football, so that it is parallel to the left ski – and you'll now be facing the opposite way.

Its best to practice this on flat ground before trying it on steep slopes or in confined spaces as its quite an awkward and tricky little manoeuvre.

POWDER TIPS

- *A good place to practice powder skiing is on the side of pistes, where the snow remains ungroomed, although it will get tracked out quickly on a good powder day.*
- *Look for relatively steep, open slopes when skiing powder. Deep powder will slow you down considerably, and you need the space to practice those wide, almost languid turns.*
- *Check the snow carefully before you venture off-piste. What looks like perfect powder from a distance may be crusty or heavy when you get onto it. Use your ski pole to prod the snow and give you information on the quality and nature of deeper layers.*
- *Watch out for lumps and bumps in the snow – these may mask hidden objects such as tree stumps and rocks.*
- *Avoid gentle slopes in deep powder as it's hard to maintain your momentum without a decent pitch to the slope.*
- *Consider using powder leashes on your skis to prevent losing them if you fall in deep powder. If you do lose your skis, use your ski poles to probe for them.*
- *Your ski jacket probably has a powder skirt – now is the time to use it! Ensure that all zippers and Velcro fastenings are closed and that you're wearing goggles rather than sunglasses, because a fall in powder will result in snow working its way into everything.*

OFF-PISTE AND POWDER

Off-piste skiing and powder are often taken to mean one and the same thing, but this is not necessarily the case. You won't always find powder off-piste, although this is generally where you will find the best of it. But, in addition to powder, you may also encounter almost every other type of snow and every kind of terrain – remember, there will have been no snowcats grooming it and there are no piste maps to advise you where to go.

From steep chutes to mellow, open powder fields, glaciers, trees, ice and crust, off-piste skiing can offer a huge variety of snow and terrain in the course of a single run, so it goes without saying that this is the playground of very competent, experienced skiers.

Recent developments in ski design (see 'powder skiing' page 95) have made the back country more accessible than ever, and less experienced skiers can now head beyond resort boundaries and test themselves in terrain that, until a few years ago, was the exclusive preserve of experts. However, although the new, fat skis make things easier than they've ever been, you might struggle to master off-piste terrain. Bear in mind that when you see skiers in these areas, they are probably locals who have taken years to reach this standard. Since most of us only get one or two weeks a year on the snow, it's unrealistic and unfair on yourself to aspire to their levels of skill.

Powder skiing

When you make your first controlled, flowing run in deep powder, you'll understand what all the fuss is about. Good powder is a magical substance and skiing it is addictive. But, like any good thing, it doesn't come easy, nor is it easy to find. And to ski it successfully requires you to forget a lot of what you've learnt about all other forms of skiing.

We'll assume you're already on a pair of wide/fat powder skis as you head off-piste, but if you try to turn by applying pressure to the inside edge of your downhill ski, as you would on-piste, you'll soon find yourself taking a tumble. This is because your turning ski will sink into the deep, soft snow whilst your unweighted ski floats up above it, throwing you off balance. To overcome this requires you to centre your weight evenly over the waist of both skis, neither leaning forward nor back, at the same time spreading your arms wider than usual to further improve your balance.

You need to turn with both feet at the same time, using an upward motion of the body to initiate the turn and take weight off the skis. This isn't easy at first because it goes against all you've learnt about weighting and unweighting your skis and using their edges, but it's the only way to ski powder.

Your arms should be held more in front of you than they would be with regular piste skiing, and you can use one arm and then the other as a fulcrum to help with the turns, and try to get into a rhythm; as you turn you'll sink deeper into the snow, so unweight coming out of the turn and it'll help with the transition into the next turn. It's best to start off with long, arcing turns at first, making them tighter as you build your skill and experience.

Powder skiing can be a magical experience.

OTHER OFF-PISTE OPTIONS
Tree skiing

Tree skiing is challenging, but is a good option in bad light and/or stormy conditions when wide, open pistes may be unskiable due to poor visibility, high winds or avalanche danger.

Some resorts, such as Sun Peaks in British Columbia, have gladed many of their runs so that the trees are spaced at varying distances to suit different skier abilities – for example, blue runs with widely spaced trees offer a great and not too challenging introduction to tree skiing. Other resorts, such as Red Resort, also in British Columbia, are famed for their steep, deep tree skiing where, on some slopes, even the locals have difficulty finding and repeating the same line through the trees.

The skill level required to ski trees obviously depends on how tightly packed the trees are, but even in well-spaced glades you need to have good control over your skis and to be able to stop very quickly (in an argument between a skier and a Douglas fir, it'll be the tree that comes out on top every time).

If you have the skills to make tight, controlled turns and decide to head for the trees, one of the prime things to remember is to anticipate several turns ahead and look for the gaps in the trees – then aim for the gap. If you see only trees, and moreover see them as intimidating obstacles, its more likely that you'll hit one. There's a certain amount of psychology involved in this approach, but it does work.

It's common sense to wear a helmet when tree skiing, and you should also remove the wrist straps from your poles in case they get caught on a branch or tree trunk.

Back country alternatives

The original style of skiing – hiking out into the back country under your own steam – is now enjoying the biggest renaissance since ski lifts were invented. This is largely due to improved, more user-friendly skis, bindings and supplementary equipment, from avalanche rescue transceivers to GPS systems and lightweight, hi-tech ski wear.

These 'niche' branches of the sport are the realm of experienced skiers. In most cases, these alternatives are undertaken with either excellent knowledge of the terrain being skied, or with a ski or mountain guide.

Telemark skiing Named after the Norwegian location where it was invented, telemark skiing involves the use of skis with bindings that only fasten at the toe and require the skier to turn by bending the knee of their downhill leg and following it around the arc of the turn with their uphill leg, also bent.

The boots are flexible, allowing the heel to lift free of the ski, hence it's also known as 'freeheel' skiing. This also allows telemarkers to climb snow slopes. Skins are attached to the bottom of the skis – these are strips of adhesive-backed fabric, which fasten to the bottom of the ski and on which the nap slides over the snow as the ski moves forward, but catches against it and stops dead when sliding backwards, allowing upward progress. They're called skins because they were originally made from sealskin.

Rather than use ski poles, true telemark enthusiasts use a traditional single pole 1.2–2 m (4–7 ft) in length, called a lurk, dragging the ends in the snow to assist with turning. Telemarking is a lovely style of skiing to watch when practised by an expert, but one of the most strenuous and difficult forms of skiing to learn.

Ski mountaineering/ski randonnée/ski touring

Ski mountaineers and ski tourers also use skis with bindings that are loose at the heel to facilitate climbing. In this case, a rigid boot much like a standard ski boot remains attached to the binding at the toe, but can be unclipped at the heel for climbing. The boot heel sits higher on the ski thanks to drop-down 'heel lifts' on the binding designed to reduce pressure on the calves on ascents. Once again skins are used to allow the ski to grip the snow on ascents. For descending, the rear of the binding is locked down and the skier rides downhill using standard alpine techniques. Randonnée is simply the French word for the sport.

Ski racing

Although there isn't scope in this book to cover the techniques involved in the various branches of ski racing, it is possible to get into racing at every level, from beginner upwards.

Many resorts have ski race courses where, for a fee, you can be timed over the course, either against another skier or against yourself. Some resorts also offer racing clinics for all levels of recreational skier. However, if you want to get into racing in a big way, it is best to join a ski club that organizes events and competitions throughout the season for different ages and the various categories.

Tree skiing in the back country.

KEEPING FIT

SKIING WILL GET YOU FIT IF YOU DO ENOUGH OF IT, BUT IF YOU ARE REASONABLY FIT BEFORE YOU START YOU'LL HAVE A BETTER TIME ON THE SLOPES AND ALSO BE LESS LIKELY TO SUFFER INJURIES.

Certain sports complement skiing – activities such as mountain biking and running work similar muscles and also develop aerobic fitness – but any reasonably strenuous exercise that's done on a regular basis will benefit you when you hit the slopes.

Getting fit or maintaining fitness through an activity you enjoy is the best way to go. If you don't enjoy an activity you're less likely to stick with it.

You need to start boosting your fitness levels about eight weeks before your ski holiday. If you are not a regular exerciser, it is advisable to consult your doctor or a qualified fitness instructor before beginning any exercise programme.

Your pre-skiing programme should involve building up muscular strength and endurance, particularly in the legs and core muscles; aerobic training, which will help you to ski longer and cope better with the effects of altitude; and stretching, which will improve flexibility and help prevent aches, strains and injuries.

Since skiing involves short, intense bursts of activity followed by longish 'rests' on the ski lift, interval work is a complementary form of training, particularly running, cycling and rowing. (Interval work combines repeated bouts of aerobic exercise interspersed with

rest periods.) Also worth considering are Swiss ball exercises; not only is this an appropriately named piece of gear for ski training, but there are few better ways of developing core muscle strength, stability and balance. There are hundreds of different exercises using a Swiss ball, but it is important to get specialist instruction in how to use one correctly.

This chapter features a selection of training exercises aimed specifically at skiers. However, if you are serious about getting fit for the sport, consult a qualified fitness instructor. A personalized training programme for you tailored to your own level of fitness and your strengths and weaknesses should also take into account what you hope to achieve on the slopes – a beginner obviously has different requirements and expectations to an advanced skier, for instance.

Don't overdo any exercise regime, especially if you're not used to it – a full circuit of exercises twice a week with at least two days rest between sessions should be adequate and will probably still leave you aching afterwards. But, by having aching muscles now, you'll be less likely to ache all over and feel tired after a day on the slopes – and the less tired you are, the better you'll ski.

WARMING UP, COOLING DOWN AND STRETCHING

It's important to warm up and stretch before skiing and to cool down and stretch afterwards if you want to minimize aches and pains and prevent muscle strains and tears. Here are a few tips before you start touching your toes:

• Don't overstretch or 'bounce' into stretches, as you can damage your muscles.

• Ideally you should perform the stretches just before you start skiing, but this isn't always easy on the mountain, especially if the stretch involves lying down in the snow. Going through a stretching routine in your hotel room is better than nothing, but try to do some stretches immediately before you start skiing in order to minimize the risk of injury.

• Do some simple stretches (e.g. upper calf stretch) throughout the day – whilst waiting in lift queues, hanging around at a ski lodge, or taking a break on the slopes.

• Although it is tempting to collapse after a hard day on the slopes, resist! Before you go for a well-deserved hot shower, spend five minutes loosening muscles and stretching tired legs and arms.

Stretching your muscles before skiing will help to avoid injuries.

Warming up

Do these exercises for around 20–30 seconds each before you go into a stretching routine.

Squatting – Squat down on your skis like a downhill racer. This is good for your lower back muscles.

Arm raise – Raise both arms above your head to stretch the upper back and shoulder muscles.

Leg swings – Swing the leg backwards and forwards. This stretches the upper thighs and gluteus maximus muscles (your buttocks).

Hip circles – Stand with your feet hip distance apart and, while attempting to keep your head centred above your feet, move your hips in a circle.

Jogging or running on the spot.

Squatting

Arm raises

Leg swings (1)

Leg swings (2)

Hip circles (1)

Hip circles (2)

Stretching

Extend the stretch until you feel a comfortable pull on the muscle rather than a painful strain. Don't overstretch, as this can do more harm than good.

Hold each stretch for 20 seconds, and try to do all of them at least once, both before and after skiing. It will take less than three minutes. However, it is better to repeat the stretches two or three times each.

Inner leg/lower back

Upper calf

Lower calf

Hamstring

Inner leg

Upper calf

Weight training

The quadriceps (thighs) are the main muscles used in skiing, but you should aim to do a full body work-out since most of your other muscles will also come into play.

Upper body exercises include:

Press-ups (try to keep a straight line through your back) – normal (1), wide arm (2) and close hands (thumbs touching) (3).

Sit ups for the abdominal muscles – normal (4), alternate elbows to knees (not shown) and alternate hand to foot (5).

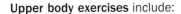

Lower body exercises should include workouts for the quads (6, 7, 12), calf muscles (10), inner thighs (adductor muscles) (8), hamstrings (9, 11) and gluteus maximus (buttock muscles) (6).

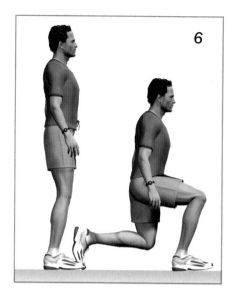

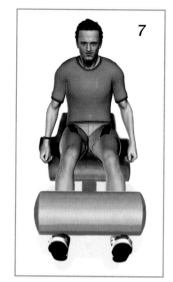

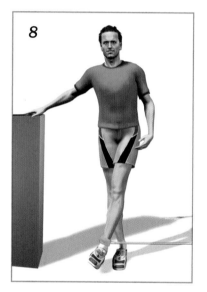

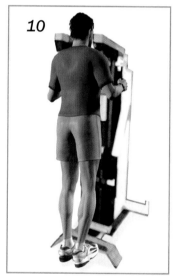

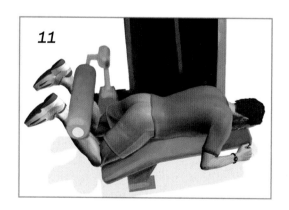

SKIING BEFORE YOU GO

If you have access to a dry ski slope and/or indoor ski dome, where artificial snow is created in a temperature-controlled environment, you don't even have to wait until you're on the white stuff to get a feel for skiing.

Indoor runs are very short in comparison with a real ski slope and, whatever their promoters may say, the surface of a dry ski slope doesn't really feel like snow (although it does allow skis to perform in much the same way as they will on a groomed piste); also, when you fall, it can hurt rather more than falling on snow, since the surface is harder (so any exposed flesh is liable to suffer grazing).

On the plus side, however, dry slope skiing can provide first-timers with a real feel for their skis and what they can do. You can learn how to use a drag lift and get used to all the paraphernalia of skis, boots, poles, etc. before your first trip to a real ski resort. This can speed up the learning process when you're in the mountains. Dry slopes also give experienced skiers the opportunity to get their ski legs back before heading out to the slopes, and perhaps help to overcome those 'first-day blues' when your skis seem to be doing a completely different thing to what your mind is asking of them.

In recent years, the advent of snow domes has presented a more 'life like' option. Man-made snow never feels quite the same as real snow but, unlike

Indoor runs are usually very short, but they are better than nothing in the summer months.

dry slopes, you're at least skiing on 'snow' and can get closer to the sensation of the real thing.

Where both dry ski slopes and ski domes really score is with their terrain parks (areas where skiers and snowboarders can 'play' on pipes, rails and so on). You don't need a huge amount of space to build a terrain park and many skiers and snowboarders from non-alpine countries have been able to develop the skills to compete against the best in the world thanks to the experience they've gained in terrain parks, which is easily adapted to real snow once they're in the mountains.

Bear in mind, though, that if your skills have been developed in terrain parks, on dry slopes or in snow domes, you may be technically proficient but you'll still need to learn about the hazards and dangers of the mountains – so don't be overconfident when you hit the mountains for the first time.

Man-made snow isn't quite the same as the real thing, but is good to practise on.

SUMMER SKIING

If you can't get through the summer months without your fix of skiing, there are plenty of options available, although summer skiing is naturally limited compared to what's available in the winter. Some high altitude resorts keep a few lifts open for skiing, usually on glaciers: the Stubai Glacier in Austria's Tyrol region, La Grand Motte above Tignes in France, and Blackcomb Glacier at Whistler in Canada are examples.

As the sun climbs in the sky each day, the snow can become very wet and heavy, but at the same time, you may be able to ski in a t-shirt and you'll certainly come back with a great tan. Be careful of the summer sun at high altitudes though – slap on the sun screen and keep hydrated. While it can be a real delight to ski on relatively uncrowded slopes in hot sunshine, just because it's summer doesn't mean it won't get cold up on the glaciers, and you should take almost all the clothing you'd need for a winter ski holiday, in case the weather does turn bad.

Another advantage of summer skiing is that ski resort accommodation and lift ticket rates may be cheaper than in winter. There is also the option of alternative summer activities, such as mountain biking, hiking, rock climbing and white water rafting, if you want a break from the skiing.

Don't forget that it is always winter somewhere else, so if you really must have the 'real' thing, head for the southern hemisphere where great skiing can be found in Argentina, Chile and New Zealand (see also page 139).

Summer skiing is limited but can be found.

STAYING SAFE
ON THE SLOPES

As much fun as it is, skiing can also be hazardous. However, you can do plenty to reduce the hazards, partly by using common sense and following the skiers' responsibility code (see page 68), and partly by taking time to learn about potential dangers, such as hypothermia and avalanches.

Ski patrol

Ski patrol are the professional-looking skiers wearing jackets festooned with the cross of St John, carrying a radio and backpack and skiing any and all terrain with irritating style and grace. Some of them even get to set off explosives (avalanche charges) and take their dog to work (avalanche rescue dogs). And they actually get paid for this...

Seriously though, if you have any problems on the mountain these are the people who can help. From a lost friend to an injured skier, or even just directions to the nearest restaurant or back down the mountain, ski patrol know everything about their mountain and are happy to help out. They can also provide invaluable advice on snow conditions, upcoming weather and dangerous terrain if you're planning to ski off-piste.

Follow their advice at all times; if ski patrol close a run, it's invariably for your safety. Part of their job is to ensure skiers behave sensibly on the mountain, and in some resorts they can confiscate your lift pass for reckless skiing, so behave yourself and listen to them.

Ski patrol using a rescue dog to search a fresh avalanche.

- *Ski with a guide.*
- *Never ski off-piste alone.*
- *If you have no choice but to ski a potentially unstable slope, always ski one person at a time.*
- *Have a basic understanding of what constitutes a potential avalanche slope.*
- *Carry avalanche safety equipment and know how to use it effectively in an emergency.*
- *Ensure that all your equipment is in good order and that you have emergency food, drink and clothing.*
- *Inform someone of your intended route and when you expect to be back.*
- *Check weather and snow conditions before leaving.*
- *If in doubt about any slope, don't ski it! Be prepared to turn back – there is no shame in turning around if snow or weather conditions are dangerous.*
- *Take a mobile phone along in case of emergency, but don't rely on it; the chances are you won't get a signal in the back country, but you never know – an injured companion of mine was once helicoptered off the mountain thanks to a member of our party who got a phone signal by climbing to the top of the highest peak around us.*
- *Ensure that your insurance covers you for off-piste skiing – you may have to get specialist cover.*

Back country/off-piste travel – the risk of avalanches

Although avalanches are primarily of concern to back country skiers, they can happen wherever there's a slope of the right angle with enough accumulated snow on it.

After a heavy snowfall, resorts may close some runs until they've been cleared of avalanche danger. You'll not be allowed to ski the affected slopes, which will be roped off and have warning signs advising of the danger.

Take heed of these signs – it takes a special kind of idiot to head out into avalanche terrain when they've been warned against it. This also applies to off-piste areas that may be permanently closed due to a constant avalanche risk – the warning signs are there for your own good, so obey them!

Back country skiing – exciting, but not without its risks.

Avalanche safety equipment

If you plan to ski the back country on a regular basis, it makes excellent sense to enrol on an avalanche safety course which, apart from teaching you survival techniques, will ensure that you are familiar with the appropriate safety gear. Specialist equipment may not stop you from getting caught in an avalanche, but it can do a lot to help you survive.

A **transceiver** is a radio device worn around your chest or waist that helps rescuers locate you if you're buried by an avalanche. It should be switched to transmit as soon as you head into the mountains and left on until the day's end.

An **avalanche probe** is a lightweight sectional pole, much like a tent pole, that assembles to 2–3 m (6.5–10 ft) in length and is used to determine quickly the exact location of a buried skier once the transceiver has located their general position under the snow.

A lightweight **collapsible shovel**, which can be attached to the back of your pack, is used to dig out a buried person.

A **clinometer** is a useful little tool which measures slope angle and can indicate slopes that may be avalanche-prone.

Avalanche survival

If you're caught in an avalanche, the standard advice is to 'swim' in the hope of staying as high as possible in the moving snow. It seems to work – it's exactly what I did on the one occasion I was caught in a slide, although I wouldn't actually call it swimming so much as frantic flailing with my arms and legs, but it seemed to keep me on the surface of the avalanche – and avoiding burial is vital since most avalanche victims die of asphyxiation within a few minutes of being buried.

Avalanche tranceiver.

Avalanche shovel with detachable handle.

Avalanche probes.

- *The most common types of avalanche are loose snow and slab avalanches.*
- *Loose snow (or point release) avalanches generally occur on slopes of over 35 degrees and start from a single point, picking up more snow as they progress downslope.*
- *Loose snow avalanches are usually less dangerous than slab avalanches and are more likely to carry you a short way downslope in a fall of snow than bury you.*
- *Slab avalanches most commonly happen on slopes between 30 and 45 degrees (ironically the kind of angle that many back country skiers are looking to descend).*
- *A slab avalanche occurs when a block of snow breaks away from the underlying snow due to a poor bond between layers of snow crystals.*
- *Slab avalanches can measure just a few feet across and slide only a few feet, or be hundreds of feet across with paths of several thousand feet, but either size could bury and kill you.*
- *Most slab avalanches are caused by humans (or animals) moving across an unstable slope and triggering the slide.*
- *Convex slopes tend to avalanche more frequently than concave.*
- *Gullies in avalanche country should be treated with caution – if a slide starts it will funnel down the gully, and there's no way of skiing out of its path.*
- *Look out for obvious signs of avalanche terrain such as trees with broken branches on the uphill side and old avalanche debris at the bottom of a slope.*
- *Listen to the snow – if you hear a heart stopping 'whump!' beneath your feet, this is from layers of unstable snow collapsing under your weight and it means you're on a potential avalanche slope – get off fast!*

If you can't get to the surface, then, as you feel the avalanche starting to slow down, try to put one arm across your face to create a breathing space and also try to spit out any snow which has forced its way into your mouth. Raise the other hand to what you think is the surface – if you can get it out of the snow it'll help you be rescued much more quickly. If you're not too deeply buried you could try yelling, but sound travels very poorly in snow and it's unlikely you'll be heard.

If one of your party gets caught in an avalanche, try to mark the spot you last saw them, as it will give you some idea of where to start your search. Look for pieces of clothing, as they may still be attached to the owner.

Rescuers should set their transceivers to receive immediately and get searching fast, since time is of the essence. However, first make sure the area you're searching is safe – you don't want to get caught in another slide yourself.

Falling

One thing is certain in skiing – you will fall. Probably more when you're a novice, but even the best skiers wipe out from time to time, especially when they're pushing themselves.

If you suffer from aches and bruises as the result of a fall, a couple of painkillers and a hot bath will no doubt see you back on the slopes the next day. You can also consider applying an ice pack to badly bruised or inflamed areas – snow placed in a plastic bag then wrapped in a towel is great for this.

The majority of falls are harmless and will probably leave you and your friends laughing, but there are ways to fall that will reduce the chance of injury. Try to fall into the slope and onto the outside of your thigh and bottom; not only is this is the shortest trajectory to the ground but you'll also be landing on the best-padded part of your anatomy! In addition, it's easier to get up from this position when you are on skis.

If you fall head first, try to let go of your poles before following the natural tendency to put your hands out in front of you; if you're still holding your poles you're more likely to suffer from skier's thumb (see page 28).

In a head-first fall, you'll come to rest with your skis uphill, so you need to swing them around and downhill in order to stand up. If this is too difficult, simply unclip and then stand up. If you're in deep powder this may be easier said than done, so to assist you, lay your poles flat on the snow in an 'X'-shape, then push down on the middle of the 'X' to push yourself up.

Few recreational skiers travel very fast. On average, the maximum speed achieved by recreational skiers is around 45 kph (28 mph). They are thus unlikely to suffer the kind of catastrophic wipe out experienced by professional ski racers. Essentially, skiing really isn't all that dangerous.

A safe fall is one that angles you into the slope and lands you on your bottom.

Injuries

You can reduce your chances of being injured by following a few common-sense rules; like not skiing beyond your ability (either in terms of terrain or speed), obeying warning signs and advice, keeping yourself well fed and watered so your energy levels remain high, and coming down off the mountain as soon as you start to feel tired – most injuries occur late in the day when exhaustion has set in.

As noted earlier (see pages 12–13), serious injuries such as breaks and fractures are rare nowadays, mainly due to the huge improvements in bindings and boots. Somewhat surprisingly though, the rate of head injuries hasn't reduced, despite a marked increase in helmet use.

Recent figures from the USA indicate that there are only 2.5 injuries for every 1,000 skier/snowboarder visits to American ski resorts. In 2002, 33 people skiing or snowboarding in the USA suffered serious injuries (head, spine, internal, etc.) whilst 39 died from ski-related accidents; a tiny fraction of the number of people on the slopes over the course of a season.

The most common 'major' injury amongst skiers is a torn anterior cruciate ligament (ACL), the ligament that helps stabilize the knee. If you tear your ACL, it will keep you off the slopes for the rest of the season, but it can return to full working order with proper treatment and physiotherapy. There has been a marked reduction in instances of ACL injuries in recent years, largely due to people using shorter skis, which don't twist and bend the knee in a fall as much as longer skis.

For the majority of skiers, the most likely 'injuries' they will suffer are bruises and strains from relatively minor spills, and muscle aches caused by doing an unfamiliar, infrequently practised activity, especially when learning or after your first couple of days of a ski vacation.

An injured skier being assisted by members of the ski patrol.

If someone suffers a serious injury, there are a few basic things to do immediately:

- *Make sure the casualty is breathing. If not, administer EAR (expired air respiration, also often called artificial respiration).*
- *Taking care to protect the spine and neck, turn the patient onto his/her side to reduce the risk of choking.*
- *If you suspect a broken limb, protect it from movement. Don't try to remove ski boots as they can actually act as a splint.*
- *Bind any wounds using a scarf or handkerchief if bandages are not available.*
- *If the casualty is in shock, try to keep the head slightly lower than the feet.*
- *Keep the casualty warm but don't give them anything to eat or drink.*
- *Secure the area – place a pair of skis in a cross on the slope well above the injured skier to warn other skiers to avoid the area.*
- *Contact ski patrol and provide the location of the accident and details of the injury.*
- *Keep the casualty informed of how the rescue is progressing.*
- *Keep the casualty alert and awake by talking to them. Ask them questions, talk about their family – anything you can think of to keep them conscious for as long as possible.*

Hypothermia

If you dress using the layering system described earlier (see page 30) and eat and drink properly whilst on the slopes, there's no reason why you should ever suffer from hypothermia whilst skiing; indeed the vast majority of skiers never do.

However, you never know when a mishap may occur that leads to the onset of hypothermia, from an off-piste fall to being stuck on a broken ski lift in bad weather. It pays to know the signs of hypothermia and what to do if you think you, or a skiing companion, may be suffering from it.

Hypothermia occurs when the core of your body loses heat faster than it produces it. The colder your core becomes, the harder it is to warm it up again, so it's important to recognize heat loss as soon as possible. Early signs of hypothermia include feeling cold and clumsy, and not doing obvious things such as putting on an extra layer, followed by apathy and listlessness. Shivering is likely but it doesn't always occur. This is followed by stumbling, lack of co-ordination, and personality changes such as becoming irrational or belligerent. Most people who have hypothermia are not aware of the fact; you are more likely to recognize it in someone else.

Treat the early stages by warming the casualty; add extra clothing or wrap them in a blanket, administer hot drinks, and encourage the casualty to move around. Most importantly, get the patient off the mountain and into a warm environment.

Do not allow someone with signs of hypothermia to continue skiing after being 'warmed up', as this could result in a relapse later in the day. Also, the initial stages of hypothermia can come across as intoxication – a good reason not to have that extra beer or schnapps at lunchtime.

If hypothermia develops to an advanced stage, where the victim is unable to stand or communicate intelligibly and may even lose consciousness, you need to take rapid action. The patient needs to be evacuated from the mountain under medical supervision as soon as possible, and kept under medical care until a full recovery has been made. Finally, always remember that it is still possible to relapse into hypothermia up to 48 hours after recovery. Keep an eye on any victims until you are sure they have suffered no ill-effects.

Cover up as much of your skin as possible to avoid suffering from frostnip or frostbite.

Frostbite

Frostbite occurs when body tissue freezes. It only happens in sub-zero temperatures and is more likely if you're dehydrated and it is windy. Extremities such as toes, fingers, nose and ears are most commonly affected by frostbite, which is manifested by the affected area appearing white or grey and feeling cold and hard.

You should be able to sense the danger signals of impending frostbite, which is a loss of feeling in the affected part. As soon as you feel this (or don't feel it to be precise), or if your extremities just feel extremely cold, get off the mountain without delay. Interim measures include warming the affected part/s by placing them against a warm area of skin, such as your armpits. Your armpits won't like it much but your fingers will; if it's your toes that are suffering you'll have to find a friend's armpits instead (which is when you discover who your real friends are!). Once off the mountain, warm the affected area in hot water (between 38 and 41°C) until completely thawed. Large blisters may occur over the affected area after warming and it's important not to burst these, as infection can set in. Seek medical attention without delay.

Frostnip

Recreational skiers are far more likely to suffer from frostnip than frostbite. It affects exposed skin in sub-zero windy conditions, most often the cheeks, nose and ears. The outer layer of skin becomes frozen and turns white, but it can be easily warmed up by putting a warm hand over the affected area to protect it from the wind. Contact frostbite is caused by touching a cold metal object, such as a chairlift, with bare hands.

SKI
RESORTS

ANY LIST OF TOP RESORTS WILL INEVITABLY BE CONTENTIOUS. HOWEVER, THIS BRIEF SELECTION AIMS TO COVER A REASONABLY WIDE RANGE OF RESORTS THAT, AMONGST THEM, HAVE SOMETHING TO OFFER EVERYONE FROM COMPLETE BEGINNER TO SEASONED EXPERT.

EUROPE

AUSTRIA

Kitzbühel

In pure skiing terms there are better resorts, but if you're looking for a traditional alpine setting and decent skiing then Kitzbühel is as good a choice as any. Beginners and intermediates in particular will have a ball on the Kitzbüheler Horn and the Hahnenkamm (famed for its World Cup downhill course), and the enjoyable signposted Ski Safari (not for total novices, though). The attractive medieval town is lovely to wander around and has plenty of nightlife too. The only downside is the limited amount of challenging terrain for experienced skiers.

Ski resorts such as Zermatt, in Switzerland, offer great skiing and fantastic scenery.

VITAL STATISTICS

Resort altitude: *760 m (2,500 ft)*
Vertical: *1,240 m (4,070 ft)*
Lifts: *57 in linked area*
Pistes: *150 km (93 miles) in linked area (40% beginner, 46% intermediate, 14% advanced/expert)*
Linked and/or neighbouring resorts: *Aurach, Jochberg, Kirchberg, Pass Thurn, Reith, Söll, St Johan in Tyrol*
Season: *Early December – late April (note that snow cover is not assured early and late season)*
Nearest airport: *Salzburg (1.5 hrs), Innsbruck (2 hrs), Munich (2.5 hrs)*
Nearest train station: *Kitzbühel*
Road: *Off the A12 Munich – Innsbruck autobahn*
Contact details: *Tel. 0043 5356 777, www.kitzbuehel.com*

St Anton

St Anton has a proud ski history – the Arlberg region in which it is situated is where early ski teaching methods were developed. The mountains here offer some of the most challenging skiing in the world, so St Anton is more of a place for novice skiers to aspire towards than to visit early in their ski career. More experienced skiers will love the fantastic array of on- and off-piste challenges available, and after dark you'll find a reasonably attractive alpine town with plenty of après-ski action, from excellent restaurants to bars and clubs.

St Anton offers challenging skiing and a lively night-life.

FRANCE

Avoriaz and the Portes du Soleil region

Avoriaz makes up part of the vast Portes du Soleil ski area (on the French/Swiss border, south of Geneva). With some 650 km (404 miles) of inter-linked pistes, if you can't find something here to excite you then you might as well give up! The resort is renowned for its wide, open cruiser runs to which novice and intermediate skiers flock, but there's plenty of very good off-piste for better skiers who want to explore. The 1960s wood-clad apartments that make up Avoriaz town won't appeal to all, but the skiing surely will, especially if you like to get some distance under your belt, with easy options of skiing into the numerous linked resorts, some of which are over the border in Switzerland – remember to take your passport!

VITAL STATISTICS

Resort altitude: 1,800 m (5,600 ft)

Vertical: 1,466 m (4,810 ft)

Lifts: 207 (Portes du Soleil area)

Pistes: 150 km (93 miles) in Avoriaz (62% beginner, 27% intermediate, 10% advanced/expert); 650 km (404 miles) in Portes du Soleil

Linked and/or neighbouring resorts: Abondance, Champéry, Champoussin, La Chapelle d'Abondance, Châtel, Les Crosets, Les Gets, Montriond, Morgins, Morzine, St Jean d'Aulps, Torgon, Val d'Illiez.

Season: Mid December – late May

Nearest airport: Geneva (2 hrs)

Nearest train station: Cluses – 40 km (25 miles), Thonons les Bains – 43 km (27 miles)

Road: Exit 18 off Autoroute Blanche at Cluses

Contact details: Tel. 0033 450 74 02 11, www.avoriaz.com

Chamonix

Chamonix is one of the oldest ski resorts in the world, but age hasn't dulled it. The huge bulk of Mont Blanc and spectacular needle-like peaks, such as the Aiguille du Midi, that soar over the town present challenges that the world's most extreme skiers struggle to conquer. For competent intermediate skiers, there's the 22 km (13.5 mile) glacier run of the Vallée Blanche. The string of resorts that make up the Chamonix experience all have plenty of runs for beginners, but this is where expert skiers can test just how good they are, whilst the rest of us enjoy skiing amongst some of the most spectacular mountainscapes in Europe. It is not possible to ski between the resorts in this area. However, they are linked by bus. Travel between them can be a bit slow, so consider taking your car, or hiring one, if you plan to ski at more than one resort.

The express cable car link between Les Arcs and La Plagne has created a huge skiing area.

VITAL STATISTICS

Resort altitude: *1,035 m (3,396 ft)*
Vertical: *2,807 m (9,210 ft)*
Lifts: *46*
Pistes: *150 km (52% beginner, 36% intermediate, 12% advanced/expert), including the resorts of Le Brévent, La Flégère, Grands Montets and Le Tour, all of which are covered by the area lift pass*
Linked and/or neighbouring resorts: *Les Houches, Megève, St-Gervais (all France), Courmayeur (Italy)*
Season: *Early December – early May*
Nearest airport: *Geneva (1 hr)*
Nearest train station: *Chamonix*
Road: *Autoroute Blanche gives excellent access to the town*
Contact details: *Tel. 0033 450 53 00 24, www.chamonix.com*

Les Arcs

The huge ski area of Les Arcs was recently expanded with an express cable car link to La Plagne to create the Paradiski area, one of the world's biggest. With this size comes the ability to offer world-class skiing to every level of skier from complete beginner to expert, and it's doubtful that anyone could cover all there is to ski here on one visit – or indeed several. On the downside, the architecture is lacking in alpine charm on the whole (with the exception of outlying villages such as Le Pré), and the nightlife is not as good as you might expect. However, if all you want to do is ski, Les Arcs is for you.

VITAL STATISTICS

Resort altitude: 1,600–2,000 m (5,250–6,562 ft); several villages at different levels make up Les Arcs as a whole

Vertical: 2,026 m (6,647 ft)

Lifts: 141 (Paradiski area)

Pistes: 200 km (124 miles) in Les Arcs ski area (5% beginner, 56% intermediate, 27% advanced, 12% expert) and a total of 425 km (264 miles) in Paradiski area

Linked and/or neighbouring resorts: Bourg St Maurice, Peisey-Nancroix, La Plagne, Le Pré, Vallandry, Villaroger. St Foy, La Rosiere, Tignes and Val d'Isere are all within a 45–60 minute drive

Season: Early December – late April/early May

Nearest airport: Chambéry (2 hrs), Geneva (2.5 hrs), Lyon (2.5 hrs)

Nearest train station: Bourg St Maurice (serves Eurostar service from London)

Road: Autoroute to Albertville from where resort is signposted

Contact details: Tel. 0033 479 07 12 57, www.lesarcs.com

Val d'Isère

If ever a resort could claim to provide something for everyone then it's Val d'Isère, with magnificent skiing, particularly for intermediate to advanced skiers, a superb lift system, frenzied nightlife if you want it, and easy links to the neighbouring high-level resort of Tignes (a better option for beginners) at 2,100 m (6,890 ft). It is not the most attractive of resorts but most people visit 'Val' for its almost endless skiing options. It is popular with British skiers, who almost outnumber their French counterparts. Many skiers visit Val d'Isere once and then never go anywhere else, so extensive are the skiing opportunities.

VITAL STATISTICS

Resort altitude: 1,850 m (6,070 ft)
Vertical: 1,906 m (6,253 ft)
Lifts: 97 including Tignes (the two areas together are known as L'Espace Killy)
Pistes: 300 km (186 miles) in L'Espace Killy (15% beginner, 50% intermediate, 35% advanced/expert)
Linked resort: Tignes. Within 45 mins drive are St Foy, Les Arcs, La Plagne and La Rosière)
Season: End November – early May
Nearest airport: Chambéry (2 hrs), Lyon (2.5 hrs), Geneva (1 hr)
Nearest train station: Bourg St Maurice (45 mins)
Road: Autoroute to Albertville, then follow signs for Moûtiers and Bourg St Maurice
Contact details: Tel. 0033 479 06 06 60, www.valdisere.com

Val d'Isère has some of the best skiing in the world.

ITALY

Courmayeur

Located on the 'opposite side' of Mont Blanc to Chamonix, Courmayeur has pretty much all you could need in a ski resort: good skiing for all abilities (especially intermediates), an attractive old alpine town, spectacular mountain scenery, good bars and renowned restaurants. About the only downside is the relatively short length of the pistes, but experienced skiers can get around that by challenging themselves on the off-piste areas, the Vallée Blanche beneath Mont Blanc or even with the local heliskiing operations. The resort's mountain restaurants are amongst the best, since the local Italian clientele places as much emphasis on good dining as good skiing.

Courmayeur has breathtaking mountain scenery.

Selva Gardena

Selva Gardena has good skiing for all standards, great restaurants, but above all some of the most beautiful mountain scenery in the world. The limestone peaks of the Dolomites soar above the slopes and when they turn every shade of purple, mauve, golden yellow and pink in the evening sun there's nothing else on earth to compare. Intermediate skiers who like to cover the ground will love the Sella Ronda Circuit. It takes you on a lift-assisted tour of neighbouring resorts and, with the region's Dolomiti Superski lift pass, you have the potential to ski some 1,220 km (758 miles) of piste in what is touted as the world's largest ski area. Of course, there's no way you'll do it in anything less than a season, but you'll certainly have fun trying.

The resort of Selva Gardena has good skiing and outstanding scenery.

SWITZERLAND

Verbier

One of the world's most famous resorts, but best left to experienced skiers who will revel in the fantastic on- and off-piste options available here (if they can work out the confusing piste map, that is!). The off-piste, in particular, is what brings expert skiers to Verbier, but intermediate level skiers will also enjoy the resort, especially Savolèyres mountain. However, novice skiers will probably be somewhat daunted by the resort's challenging slopes. The après-ski is renowned, although Verbier is popular with well-heeled punters so don't expect a cheap night out, or a cheap ski holiday.

VITAL STATISTICS

Resort height: *1,500 m (4,921 ft)*

Vertical: *1,830 m (6,004 ft)*

Lifts: *94*

Pistes: *150 km (93 miles) in Verbier, 410 km (255 miles) in linked Four Valleys area (33% beginner, 42% intermediate, 6% advanced, 19% expert)*

Linked and/or neighbouring resorts: *Bruson, Champex-Lac, Nendaz, Siviez, Thyon, La Tzoumaz, Veysonnaz*

Season: *November – late April*

Nearest airport: *Geneva (2 hrs)*

Nearest train station: *Le Châble (15 mins drive)*

Road: *Motorway Geneva – Lausanne – Martigny, then via a steep mountain road to the resort*

Contact details: *Tel. 0041 27 775 3888, www.verbier.ch*

Verbier is the ideal resort for intermediate-level and experienced skiers.

Zermatt

Undoubtedly one of the world's finest ski resorts, the truly gorgeous alpine scenery alone is enough to attract you to Zermatt, sitting as it does at the base of the mighty Matterhorn. On top of that, the car-free town has plenty of character and the skiing is excellent for most skiers, especially beginners and advanced. Although about half the runs in Zermatt are graded intermediate they can be quite challenging for weaker intermediate level skiers, especially in icy and/or crowded conditions. There's also the option to ski over to Cervinia in Italy, one of Europe's most snow-sure resorts and great for beginners and intermediates. For gourmands, Zermatt's mountain restaurants are renowned for their menus and their views of the Matterhorn.

The Klein Matterhorn Cablecar with the Matterhorn in the background.

VITAL STATISTICS

Resort height: *1,620 m (5,315 ft)*

Vertical: *2,279 m (7,477 ft)*

Lifts: *62 including Cervinia (a ski pass for both resorts is available)*

Pistes: *200 km (124 miles) Zermatt, 400 km (250 miles) including Cervinia (10% beginner, 54% intermediate, 36% advanced/expert)*

Linked and/or neighbouring resorts: *Crans Montana, Grächen, Riederalp, Saas-Fee (Switzerland), Cervinia (Italy)*

Season: *Late November/early December – late April/early May (summer skiing available at Klein Matterhorn)*

Nearest airport: *Sion (1.5 hrs), Geneva (4 hrs)*

Nearest train station: *Zermatt*

Road: *Drive as far as Täsch, then train to Zermatt*

Contact details: *Tel. 0041 27 966 8100, www.zermatt.ch*

EUROPE – THE BEST OF THE REST

The short directory listed so far only scratches the surface of the immense number of skiing options available in Europe. There are plenty of other world-class resorts throughout the Alps, such as charming village of Alpbach in Austria, family-friendly Megève in France, beginner to intermediate favourite Livigno in Italy, France's intermediate magnet, Serre Chevalier and off-piste favourite Alpe d'Huez.

There are the lesser-known countries, such as Pyreneean principality Andorra which, in recent years, has had some excellent snow seasons and major resort improvements; France and Spain also have Pyreneean resorts, and further south in Spain you can ski the Sierra Nevada mountains in Mediterranean sunshine.

In Eastern Europe, resorts such as Borovets in Bulgaria and Poina Brasov in Romania provide good value and cultural alternatives, whilst Kranjska Gorja in Slovenia offers an Austrian atmosphere at budget rates. Be aware, though, that the facilities in eastern Europe are rarely as good as those in the more established alpine nations.

Scandinavia, the historical home of skiing, has some excellent resorts with a superb range of facilities both on and off the slopes, let down only by relatively low altitudes and short daylight hours in midwinter. Voss and Trysil in Norway, Åre in Sweden and Levi in Finland are good examples of Scandinavian resorts with a wonderful atmosphere, good skiing and plenty of other winter sports options, particularly Nordic skiing.

Scottish resorts, such as Aviemore, Glencoe and the Nevis Range, offer a hit and miss approach to skiing, where you may encounter everything from Arctic blizzards to perfect powder in the course of a couple of days. There are plenty of alternatives if skiing conditions are poor, from dog sledding to whisky tasting, so keep your options open and you can have a good 'winter holiday' as opposed to a 'ski holiday', whatever the conditions you find.

Alpbach in Austria is a charming and world-class ski resort.

NORTH AMERICA
USA

Alta, Utah

Alta has skiing in its blood – so much so that snow-boarders are banned. The former silver mining camp was developed as a ski resort in 1939. It holds tenaciously to its roots, with no-frills facilities (including old and ancient lifts). However, this is more than made up for by an average snowfall of 1,270 cm (500 in) of fantastic talc-dry Utah powder each winter. One of Alta's strong points is that beginners and experts alike can enjoy great skiing here, and the magnificent back country can be enjoyed on the highly recommended guide-led Ski Utah Interconnect Tour (www.skiutah.com).

Along with its reputation for expensive boutiques and celebrity clientele, Aspen also has fantastic skiing spread over four mountains.

VITAL STATISTICS

Resort height: 2,600 m (8,530 ft)

Vertical: 616 m (2,020 ft)

Lifts: 8 plus a number of drag lifts

Piste acreage/trails: 890 ha (2,200 acres). 54 trails (35% beginner, 40% intermediate, 35% expert)

Linked and/or neighbouring resorts: Brighton, Snowbird, Solitude

Season: Mid November – mid April

Nearest airport: Salt Lake City (45 min–1 hr)

Nearest train station: Salt Lake City

Road: Interstate 15 from Salt Lake City then Highway 210 up Little Cottonwood Canyon. Parking lot and shuttle service at base of canyon if you don't fancy the snaking road up to the resort

Contact details: Tel. 001 801 359 1078, www.alta.com

Aspen, Colorado

Famed as a winter haunt for the rich and famous, some of whom are more intent on ostentatious displays of wealth in the resort's expensive boutiques than actually hitting the slopes. Aspen nevertheless has wonderful skiing to suit all abilities, spread over four mountains: Ajax (for experts), Aspen Highlands (free riders), Buttermilk (great novice terrain) and Snowmass (family-friendly). Customer service on and off the mountain is impeccable and the resort offers great restaurants and shopping along with the chance to rub shoulders with Hollywood stars, but it's not the place to visit if you're on a tight budget. Note that with a summit elevation of 3,813 m (12,510 ft) at Snowmass, altitude can be a problem for some visitors.

VITAL STATISTICS

Resort height: 2,422 m (7,945 ft)
Vertical (max): 1,343 m (4,406 ft) at Snowmass Mountain
Lifts: 39
Piste acreage/trails: 1,980 ha (4,893 acres). 316 trails spread over four mountains (16% beginner, 40% intermediate, 24% advance/expert, 20% expert)
Linked and/or neighbouring resorts: None
Season: Late November – early/mid April
Nearest airport: Aspen (10 mins), Eagle County/Vail (1.5 hrs), Denver (3.5 hrs)
Nearest train station: Glenwood Springs (1 hr)
Road: From Denver to Glenwood Springs on I–70 then Hwy 82 to the resort
Contact details: Tel. 001 970 925 1220, www.aspensnowmass.com

Big Sky, Montana

You can't fail to be impressed by Big Sky's Lone Mountain which, at 3,400 m (11,166 ft), stands proud above the resort, close to the state border with Idaho and Wyoming. You'll be even more impressed by the vertiginous double black diamond runs down it. However, there are also plenty of options here for intermediate and novice skiers, and the slopes are usually quiet, with lift queues a rarity. Should you need a break from skiing, Yellowstone National Park is only 45 minutes away. The only downside is that the après-ski action at Big Sky is rather limited in comparison with many European resorts.

VITAL STATISTICS

Resort height: *2,073 m (6,800 ft)*

Vertical: *1,326 m (4,350 ft)*

Lifts: *15*

Piste acreage: *1456 ha (3,600 acres). 202 trails (17% beginner, 25% intermediate, 58% advanced/expert)*

Linked and/or neighbouring resorts: *None*

Season: *Late November – late April*

Nearest airport: *Bozeman (1 hr), Salt Lake City (5 hrs)*

Nearest train station: *None*

Road: *Eight miles up Hwy 64 off US 191*

Contact details: *Tel. 001 406 995 5000, www.bigskyresort.com*

Big Sky is seldom over-run with skiers, and is ideal for all levels of ability.

Breckenridge, Colorado

The attractive Victorian-era settlement of Brecken-ridge has good options for all standards of skier in a large and well-linked ski area, and a superb terrain park. It also has a reputation as a hard-partying town, making it one of the most popular ski resorts in the USA, so you can experience busy slopes and lift queues. If you're looking for a good-value US ski destination that will keep you busy day and night it should be a definite consideration. However, the altitude of over 2,740 m (9,000 ft) can be a problem for some (especially if you've been hitting the alcohol).

The lively nightlife at Breckenridge makes it a popular ski resort.

Jackson Hole, Wyoming

Jackson Hole houses an eclectic mix of cowboys, Hollywood glitterati, hard-core ski bums and some of the wildest piste and off-piste skiing in North America. There are good options for novice skiers, but insecure intermediates may find the options a little daunting. The infamous aerial tram to the top of Rendezvous Mountain was removed from service in 2006, but is due for replacement and offers a thrilling ride, awesome summit views and access to extremely challenging terrain. Jackson itself is a pleasant ski town which hasn't totally lost sight of its Wild West roots, although the nightlife isn't that boisterous.

Jackson Hole offers stunning scenery.

VITAL STATISTICS

Resort height: *1,924 m (6,311 ft)*

Vertical: *1,262 m (4,139 ft)*

Lifts: *10*

Piste acreage: *1,011 ha (2,500 acres)*
76 trails (10% beginner, 40% intermediate, 50% advanced/expert)

Neighbouring resorts: *Grand Targhee, Snow King*

Season: *Early December – early April*

Nearest airport: *Jackson Hole (15 mins to Jackson, 35 mins to resort), Salt Lake City (5 hrs)*

Nearest train station: *None*

Road: *From I–15 take US26 at Idaho Falls then Hwy 31, 33 and 22 to Jackson*

Contact details: *Tel. 001 307 733 2292, www.jacksonhole.com*

Mammoth Mountain, California

Just to prove that the Sunshine State isn't all beaches and palm trees, Mammoth Mountain in the Sierra Nevada range gets over ten metres (400 in) of snow a year – and an average 300 days of sunshine. Top class skiing for all abilities in an extensive resort area, great terrain parks and a very long season mean that despite its relatively remote location, Mammoth is well worth a visit. Nightlife is rather limited, however, but if you just want to ski your socks off and get a good tan at the same time, then Mammoth should be a serious consideration.

VITAL STATISTICS

Resort height: 2,424 m (7,953 ft)
Vertical: 945 m (3,100 ft)
Lifts: 27
Piste acreage: 1,416 ha (3,500 acres)
150 trails (25% beginner, 40% intermediate, 35% advanced/expert)
Neighbouring resorts: June Mountain
Season: November – June, some years as late as July
Nearest airport: Reno (3 hrs), Los Angeles (5 hrs)
Nearest train station: None
Road: I 395 from Los Angeles or Reno then Hwy 203
Contact details: Tel. 001 760 934 0745, www.mammothmountain.com

Sun Valley, Idaho

The first resort in the world to install a chair lift in 1936, Sun Valley has remained at the cutting edge in terms of visitor facilities ever since, with some of the most opulent ski lodges in North America, a superb snowmaking system (it's not called 'Sun' Valley for nothing) and a fine lift system. The resort is remote and the skiing on the main mountain (Mt Bald) can be intimidating for novices, but strong intermediates and expert skiers will love the options, and there's a separate smaller hill, Dollar Mountain, where beginners can cut their teeth. Watch out for Hollywood stars on the slopes.

As well as great skiing, Sun Valley offers ice skating, huskie rides and horse-drawn sleighs.

VITAL STATISTICS

Resort height: *1,752 m (5,750 ft)*
Vertical: *1,036 m (3,400 ft)*
Lifts: *19*
Piste acreage: *830 ha (2,054 acres)*
75 trails (36% beginner, 42% intermediate, 22% advanced/expert)
Neighbouring resorts: *None*
Season: *Thanksgiving Day – mid/late April*
Nearest airport: *Hailey (30 mins), Boise (3 hrs), Salt Lake City (5.5 hrs)*
Nearest train station: *None*
Road: *From Boise via I 84, US 20 and Hwy 75*
Contact details: *Tel. 001 208 786 8259, www.sunvalley.com*

USA – THE BEST OF THE REST

With limited space it is not possible to cover the fantastic skiing terrain of Taos and New Mexico; the equally excellent skiing of the resorts set around deep-blue Lake Tahoe in California; the wild mountains of Washington and Oregon; and the smaller, pretty resorts of the northeast such as Stowe and Smugglers' Notch. And then of course there's Alaska, with just a handful of small resorts (and several heliski operations), which have world class powder that makes the long journey north worthwhile.

CANADA

Fernie, British Columbia

Lashings of snow, uncrowded slopes to suit all standards and good-value skiing and accommodation make the relatively long transfer to Fernie from Calgary well worth the effort. Novice and intermediate skiers will discover great cruiser runs on which to hone their technique, whilst more advanced skiers are unlikely to tire of Fernie's powder-filled bowls and demanding glades and chutes. The nightlife is fairly quiet, but other than this, Fernie is definitely one of Canada, if not North America's, top ski resorts.

Fernie often enjoys fantastic powder snow and is a great resort for all levels of skier.

VITAL STATISTICS

Resort height: *1,067 m (3,500 ft)*

Vertical: *857 m (2,811 ft)*

Lifts: *9*

Piste acreage: *1,013 ha (2,504 acres)*
106 trails (30% beginner, 40% intermediate, 30% advanced/expert)

Neighbouring resorts: *None*

Season: *December – mid April*

Nearest airport: *Calgary (3.5 hrs)*

Nearest train station: *None*

Road: *A delightful drive from Calgary on Highway 22 via Crowsnest Pass*

Contact details: *Tel. 001 250 423 4655, www.skifernie.com*

Kicking Horse, British Columbia

Kicking Horse is remote and surrounded by magnificent mountains and forests. The skiing here is not really for beginners, although there are slopes to cater for them. Rather, the terrain is more suited to skiers wanting to push themselves and experience a little adventure. The bowl and tree skiing is inspirational, and the groomed runs can be equally challenging, although there's nearly always an easy way down to the base if you bite off more than you can chew. The award-winning Eagle's Eye Restaurant at the top of the mountain is a 'must' for lunch. Development is still in the early stages at Kicking Horse (it opened in 2001), but this is one to keep an eye on in the future.

VITAL STATISTICS

Resort height: 1,180 m (3,871 ft)

Vertical: 1,260 m (4,134 ft)

Lifts: 4

Piste acreage: 1,113 ha (2,750 acres)

64 trails (26% beginner, 25% intermediate, 49% advanced/expert)

Neighbouring resorts: None

Season: mid December – mid April

Nearest airport: Calgary (3 hrs)

Nearest train station: None

Road: A spectacular mountain drive from Calgary via the town of Golden at the base of the mountain

Contact details: Tel. 001 250 439 5400, www.kickinghorseresort.com

Kicking Horse is ideal for experienced skiers.

Lake Louise, Alberta

The scenery at Lake Louise is so stunning it almost takes your breath away, and the skiing is just as good. Consistent, high-quality powder falls here in the Canadian Rockies to provide great conditions on a wide range of slopes suited to everyone from beginner to expert. Be warned, however, it can get cold in mid-winter: temperatures as low as −70°C (−94°F) have been recorded at the summit! Good children's facilities, short lift queues, relatively empty slopes, and some other top resorts within easy reach all make Lake Louise an excellent ski destination.

VITAL STATISTICS

Resort height: 1,645 m (5,397 ft)
Vertical: 1,000 m (3,281 ft)
Lifts: 12
Piste acreage: 1,700 ha (4,200 acres)
113 trails (25% beginner, 45% intermediate, 30% advanced/expert)
Neighbouring resorts: Sunshine Village, Norquay
Season: November − May
Nearest airport: Calgary (2 hrs)
Nearest train station: None
Road: Lovely two hour drive from Calgary
Contact details: Tel. 001 403 762 4561, www.skibig3.com

Lake Louise − fantastic skiing and scenery to match.

Sun Peaks, British Columbia

Sun Peaks is one of the most skier-friendly places in North America, with every level of skier able to have a thoroughly good time here in what are generally excellent snow conditions. It's also within easy reach of two equally enticing resorts: Silver Star and Big White. It's worth trying to ski them all. One of the great attractions here is fun and easy glade skiing on Sundance Mountain. The small and homely resort at the base of the mountain rounds the whole thing off perfectly.

VITAL STATISTICS

Resort height: 1,125 m (3,691 ft)
Vertical: 881 m (2,890 ft)
Lifts: 8
Piste acreage: 1,413 ha (3,491 acres)
114 trails (20% beginner, 61% intermediate, 19% advanced/expert)
Neighbouring resorts: Big White, Silver Star
Season: November – April
Nearest airport: Kamloops (45 mins)
Nearest train station: Kamloops (shuttles to mountain)
Road: Four hours along Trans-Canada Highway from Vancouver
Contact details: Tel. 001 250 578 7842, www.sunpeaksresort.com

Whistler, British Columbia

This is easily Canada's best-known ski resort, and with good reason. It is huge in both area and 'vert', with dramatic mountains and glaciers and year-round skiing. Hard-partying skiers come from all over the world to Whistler and, from first-timer to world's best there's sufficient variety in the resort's 12 bowls and three glaciers. That said, Whistler isn't perfect; it's not unusual for rain rather than snow to fall at lower altitudes, since the resort lies only 80 km (50 miles) from the coast and its accordingly mild climate. It can also be very busy, both on the lifts and in the resort. In recent years it has also become quite pricey.

VITAL STATISTICS

Resort height: 675 m (2,215 ft)
Vertical: 1,609 m (2,579 ft)
Lifts: 33
Piste acreage: 2,862 ha (7,071 acres)
200 trails (18% beginner, 55% intermediate, 27% advanced/expert)
Neighbouring resorts: Grouse Mountain
Season: November – June with summer skiing on Horstman Glacier
Nearest airport: Vancouver (2 hrs)
Nearest train station: Vancouver
Road: Via the spectacular Sea to Sky Highway from Vancouver
Contact details: Tel. 001 604 664 5625, www.whistlerblackcomb.com

CANADA – THE BEST OF THE REST

Canada's eastern resorts include state-of-the-art Mont Tremblant in Quebec, which has an eclectic mix of French-Canadian culture and well-groomed slopes (but note that it can be notoriously cold and icy). Mont Sainte-Anne is renowned for spectacular views across the vast St Lawrence River and its proximity to the beautiful city of Quebec. Back over in British Columbia there are several smaller resorts, such as the tree skier's Mecca of Red Mountain and the little powder-hound magnet of Whitewater. The province is also famed for some of the most professional heli- and cat-skiing operations in the world.

THE REST OF THE WORLD

Look carefully and you'll find that most developed countries that have mountains and snow will also have ski areas of some kind. Japan has several resorts, one of which, Shiga Kogen, was host to the 1988 Winter Olympics. All Japan's resorts have heaps of character and modern facilities and offer a very different ski experience to Europe and North America.

Resorts to consider if you don't mind the long and costly journey to the southern hemisphere include Las Leñas in Argentina. It has some of the most challenging skiing in South America (which means that it's not really that good for beginners). Portillo in Chile is uncrowded, dramatic and picturesque. Mount Ruapehu in New Zealand has dramatic volcanic scenery and the longest vertical drop in Australasia. Australia also has a number of efficient, state-of-the-art ski resorts, although snow quality can be erratic, Thredbo is a popular option where, if the skiing isn't too good, the partying always is.

The bottom line is that wherever there are mountains and snow there's the potential to ski, which gives you an awful lot of the planet to go and explore.

Sun Peaks in British Columbia has pistes suitable for all skiers, whatever their level of skill.

GLOSSARY

As with any sport, there's a lot of jargon involved with skiing. Here are a few of the more mystifying words and phrases you are likely to hear on the mountain and in the bars.

angulation – Body movements to control the angle of the edge of your skis on the snow.

ACL (anterior cruciate ligament) – The most common injury in skiing is tearing the ACL, a knee ligament. The best way to reduce your chances of this happening is through developing strong legs and good ski technique.

avy/avy control – Avalanche/avalanche control. Controlled triggering of avalanches to make slopes safe, usually done with explosive charges.

backcountry skiing (North American) – Equivalent of European 'off-piste' skiing, away from lift-accessed resort skiing, beyond the resort boundary (also known as 'out of bounds skiing').

berm – Bank of snow used to provide stability on outside of a turn, especially on race courses.

black – Expert ski run in European resorts, equivalent to double black diamond in North America.

black diamond – Intermediate to advanced ski run in North America, equivalent to red in Europe.

blue – Beginner to intermediate run.

bowl – Natural basin; often traps snow.

bumps – Also known as moguls. Large rounded humps of snow on an ungroomed slope caused by skiers turning.

camber – The amount of natural bend in an unweighted ski.

carving – Smooth, clean turn using edge of ski.

cat skiing – Skiing from a snowcat which is used to access the top of the mountain.

cat track – Track used by piste basher, often an easy way down the mountain due to gentle gradient.

chute – Also known as couloir; steep, narrow gully.

cirque (French) – Deep bowl-shaped hollow at the head of a valley or on a mountain – less commonly known as a cwm (Welsh).

corduroy – Freshly groomed snow.

corn snow – Granular snow, usually occurs in spring as a result of freeze/thaw action.

cornice (French) – Overhanging mass of snow on downwind side of a ridge.

crust – Icy surface layer of snow, easily broken by weight of skier.

DIN – *Deutsche industrie normen*: a universal number used by ski manufacturers to determine the release point of bindings. Your DIN setting is related to weight, height, age and experience and will be the same on any manufacturer's bindings.

edge – Sharp metal edge on either side of ski, which cuts into snow when turning, particularly when carving. Edging is using the ski's edge to traverse across or down a slope.

fall line – The line a snowball would follow if rolled downslope; the most direct line down a ski slope.

fat skis – Wider skis for powder snow which 'float' through the snow rather than sinking.

first tracks – Left by those skiers who manage to get up in time to catch the first lift of the day.

freeride/freeski – Skiing the whole of the mountain, irrespective of the terrain encountered.

freestyle – Skiing in halfpipes and terrain parks involving lots of tricks, especially aerials.

glade skiing – Skiing through woods, which have usually been thinned out for easier access.

green – Beginner's run.

granular snow – Similar to corn snow but harder. May be found in mornings on ungroomed pistes.

grooming – Maintenance of trails with snowcats to prevent formation of moguls and provide smooth, 'corduroy' runs for carving.

halfpipe – U-shaped channel of snow with smooth, compacted sides used for freestyle tricks.

herring-bone – To climb uphill on skis using the inside edges to dig into the snow and prevent sliding backwards, leaving a herring-bone shaped trail behind.

in-bounds (North America) – Area of resort patrolled by ski patrol.

jib – Skiing on a surface other than snow, especially rails in a terrain park.

kicker – Jump with a launch ramp for bigger air.

lifties – Seasonal lift workers who make the mistake of thinking that by working on the lifts they'll get to ski a lot.

magic carpet – Surface lift in the form of a conveyor belt. Designed for complete beginners, especially children.

moguls – *See bumps.*

off-piste (European, from French) – Terrain both within and outside a resort that is not groomed.

packed powder – Snow packed down and hardened through skiing and boarding.

piste (French) – Maintained ski run, usually called trail in North America.

Poma – French ski lift manufacturer, sometimes used generically to describe a button lift.

powder – Fresh, light snow.

rail slide – Metal rail for skiers and boarders to slide down in a terrain park.

red – Intermediate to expert run.

schussing (German) – Skiing straight down the fall line without turning.

shaped ski – Skis with a marked sidecut, making them wider at the tip and tail. Good for carving.

sideslipping – Slipping down the slope with skis at 90 degrees to the fall line; often used to negotiate steep or difficult terrain.

skating – Technique like that practised on skates, used to travel across flat terrain or gain speed.

ski brake – Device attached to bindings to prevent the ski from sliding down the mountain if it comes off in a fall.

snowcat – Caterpillar vehicle used for maintaining ski runs, also known as 'piste basher' (Europe) and 'groomer' (North America).

stem Christie – A type of turn midway between a snowplough and a parallel turn.

surface lift – Lift on which you're dragged along the snow, e.g. T-bar.

T-bar – Lift shaped like an inverted 'T' that drags one or two people up the hill.

telemark skiing – Traditional Scandinavian style of skiing which uses a binding in which the heel is free to lift. Popular for backcountry skiing.

terrain park – Area set aside with jumps, obstacles and possibly a half pipe for freestyle skiing and boarding.

tracked out – Fresh snow that has been heavily skied, hence all the 'tracks'.

traverse – Zig-zagging down a slope using the whole width of the slope before each turn.

tree well – Snow hollow formed around the base of a tree – can be dangerous as often very difficult to get out of.

vertical/vert – The vertical distance between the top and bottom of a run.

waist – Mid-section of a ski.

wedge turn (North American) – Snowplough turn.

INDEX

CREDITS

Copyright rests with the individuals and/or their agencies listed below. Key: t = top; c = centre; b = bottom.

PHOTOGRAPHIC CREDITS					
Front cover	Salomon	p45	4Corners Images	p105–06	Action Images
Back cover	Getty Images	p46	John Cleare	p107	Getty Images
p2–3	skifernie.com/	p47	Bruce Rowles	p108	Venture Pix
	Henry Georgi	p48	Stockshot	p109	Stockshot
p4–5	Schöffel	p49	michigan.org	p110 t	Venture Pix
p6–7	Getty Images	p50	Bruce Rowles	p110 c	Venture Pix
p8	michigan.org	p51	Getty Images	p110 b	John Cleare
p10	Salomon	p52	Bruce Rowles	p112	Venture Pix
p11	Alpine Club Photo	p61	Stockshot	p113	Stockshot
	Library	p62	Salomon	p115	Getty Images
p13–14	Stockshot	p64 t	jacksonhole.com	p116	Stockshot
p15	skifernie.com/	p64 b	Getty Images	p118	TVB St Anton
	Henry Georgi	p65	crans-montana.ch		am Arlberg
p16	Venture Pix	p66	michigan.org	p120	Action Images
p17	adelboden.ch	p67	John Cleare	p122–24	4Corners Images
p18	Bruce Rowles	p68	michigan.org	p125	Verbier/Bagnes
p19	Stockshot	p69	Stockshot		Tourisme
p20	John Cleare	p70	Schöffel	p126	4Corners Images
p21	Stockshot	p76	Getty Images	p127	alpbach.at
p22–23	Bruce Rowles	p77	Stockshot	p128	Grafton Smith/
p24	Photolibrary	p80 t	Getty Images		Corbis
p26–35	Salomon	p80 b	John Cleare	p130	Stockshot
p36	Venture Pix	p82	Schöffel	p131	Still Pictures
p38	John Cleare	p83	Venture Pix	p132	Stockshot
p39	Getty Images	p91	Getty Images	p134	visitsunvalley.com
p40–41	Stockshot	p95	Getty Images	p135	skifernie.com/
p42	Getty Images	p97	Bruce Rowles		Henry Georgi
p43	Bruce Rowles	p98	Getty Images	p136–37	Bruce Rowles
p44	Stockshot	p100	Stockshot	p139	sunpeaksresort.com